*Coming to Terms
with the Short Story*

Coming to Terms
with the Short Story

• • • • •

SUSAN LOHAFER

LOUISIANA STATE UNIVERSITY PRESS

BATON ROUGE AND LONDON

Designer: Albert Crochet
Typeface: Linotron Galliard
Typesetter: G&S Typesetters, Inc.
Printer: Thomson-Shore, Inc.
Binder: John H. Dekker, Inc.

Publication of this book has been assisted by a grant
from the Andrew W. Mellon Foundation.

Library of Congress Cataloging in Publication Data

Lohafer, Susan.
    Coming to terms with the short story.

    Bibliography: p.
    Includes index.
    1. Short story.   I. Title.
PN3373.L56   1983   808.3'1   82-20366
ISBN 0-8071-1086-8

To my husband

Contents

• • •

Acknowledgments

• • •

Parts of this book have been on my mind ever since I heard the question, "What is prose rhythm?" I never did come up with an answer—the question still belongs to the asker—but, with the help of colleagues like Paul Byron Diehl, I found what my own questions were. Still, I might never have pursued them had they not led me soon, often, and happily to the work of William H. Gass. I am grateful to his prose for what it has taught me about fiction making. And for guidance in the general study of rhetoric and stylistics, I want to thank Carl H. Klaus and Richard Lloyd-Jones—though I value even more their friendship and encouragement. I owe also a special debt to William M. Gibson, who kindly gave me access to notes and correspondence related to his work on Kate Chopin. There would be no end to a list of students who, with persistent curiosity and lively response, have helped me keep faith with my purposes. I'll mention just two, Kathryn Etter and Terry Krueger. In the last stages of revision, I was fortunate in having the masterly advice of Charles E. May and the guidance of Arlen J. Hansen, whose comments are worth writing a book for. Where I have failed to benefit from their wisdom, the fault is entirely my own. So, too, is the responsibility for whatever errors and omissions remain in the text. Finally, I am especially thankful to the University of Iowa for two gifts of time, an Old Gold Summer Fellowship and a semester's Developmental Leave. There is, of course, no putting in words my gratitude for my family's interest and support.

*Coming to Terms
with the Short Story*

Introduction

• • •

The ever-louder thumping of a heartbeat, a waking after twenty years of sleep, a meeting with the Devil in the woods—you know where you are. In the midst of three classic American short stories. Their names, I'm sure, have come to you: "The Tell-Tale Heart," "Rip Van Winkle," "Young Goodman Brown." Were I to dwell on the sound of a muffled heartbeat, the feel of a bearded chin, the sight of pink ribbons—you wouldn't be surprised. Concrete imagery, its way of focusing attention, of growing symbolic, is part of what we've been trained to appreciate when reading short stories. And if I were to go on speaking of setting and theme, of atmosphere and tone, of plot and character, I would be doing what we've been taught to do by the anthology textbooks.

I have no quarrel with them. While some may teach a mechanical dissection, others are thoughtfully conceived, and what matters, of course, is the teacher. I'm afraid that he or she, especially on the college level, has been at a disadvantage when compared to the teacher of the novel or the poem. After all, the teacher of *Middlemarch* can read books on George Eliot, but can turn then to F. R. Leavis, to Wayne Booth, to Franz Stanzel, to numerous critics and scholars who have helped to shape what we mean by the aesthetic of the novel. On the other hand, the teacher of "Young Goodman Brown" can read books on Hawthorne, scores of articles on the story, and the editorial hints of a hundred anthologies. He or she can, of course, go to the literary histories. There is a little-known monograph, part of the Barnes and Noble Critical Idiom series, that gives a succinct review of the form. There are also the full-fledged histories of its development and master practitioners. William Peden's *The American Short Story* may be the best known; Walter Allen's *The Short Story in English* is the most recent and monumental. But where does one go to find a coherent and comprehensive theory of short fiction?

To Germany, perhaps? A good deal has been written about the formal properties of the *novelle*, and particularly about its structural affinities with drama, but also about its peculiar forms of tension (*Spannung*) as well as the importance of prose style.[1] In English, however, the closest analogues to these theories seem to be in the craft books, the "how-to" manuals and handbooks where "plot" and *"punkt"* are graphically analyzed. Most of our innovative work on the story comes, not surprisingly, in shorter forms of discourse—articles, introductions, chapters of books, essays. Charles E. May has collected many of them in *Short Story Theories*. There one can find Poe's famous review of *Twice-Told Tales*, as well as reflections by other writers of short fiction like Frank O'Connor and Eudora Welty. But there, too, one can find the beginnings of theories, of systematic inquiries—by people like Eileen Baldeshwiler and Norman Friedman—into the formal properties of short, as opposed to long, fiction. May's book is a gathering together of voices scattered over more than a hundred years and a few national boundaries. They speak in many different ways about stories and they make one realize how piecemeal, how tentative, how subsidiary, and how informal are the materials of a criticism of short fiction. The good teacher may feel liberated, in a way enfranchised. In this field there is a democracy of experts. On the other hand, there is an aristocracy of genres in which the short story is forever in the train of the novel, classified by author, subcategorized as text. For every course in "the realistic novel," how many courses, do you suppose, are taught in "the lyrical short story"?

As a reader, writer, and teacher of short stories, I have been fortunate by location. At the University of Iowa there exist strong traditions in both the training of young writers and the study of prose style. While there is no formal coordination between such necessarily private acts of mind, there is a continual excitation of interest in such matters. Many students come to Iowa to write fiction, and many of them are serious

---

1. See Cay Dollerup, "Concepts of 'Tension,' 'Intensity,' and 'Suspense' in Short-Story Theory," *Orbis Litterarum: International Review of Literary Studies* (Copenhagen), XXV, 314–37.

about short fiction because so too are many of the writers they admire —William Gass, Donald Barthelme, Flannery O'Connor, John Updike, and the list could go on. These students want to know how short fiction works, and they are not so much interested in a scholarly theory as in a practical poetics. It is at this point that I have most gladly met them. The occasions have been such courses as, indeed, "the lyrical short story," but also courses on individual writers for whom the short story is the natural and the chief form of expression. What I have brought to these occasions is not only an interest in particular writers, particular stories, but also a habit of focus, a gauging of attention to prose behavior on the level of the sentence. What must have been a natural bent in this direction has surely been reinforced by the presence at Iowa of specialists in expository theory and pedagogy, colleagues who introduced me to rhetorical theory and stylistic analysis. Let me absolve them of any responsibility for the uses—freely adapted and sometimes unorthodox—to which I've put so much I have learned from them!

For in writing about short story aesthetics I've had in mind an audience more interested in the form than in any one critical discipline. I've wanted to address readers of short stories, and in particular those who are trying to write stories of literary merit and those who are teaching classic, modern, and contemporary stories on the graduate as well as undergraduate levels. Modern criticism, with its post-Structuralist, phenomenological, semiotic, Derridean, and other interests, has been aware of the short story, off and on, as a testing ground for this or that theory of narrative. I've drawn from many of those sources, and others more traditional, to find a basis for short story criticism, to bring it to the attention of those who, more committed to individual schools or approaches, may add richness and variety to the field. For the twenty articles in May's collection, shouldn't there be twenty books in the making?

This book is just one kind of beginning. It deals in theories, but it doesn't construct one—except incidentally. As I've said, my starting point was the sentence. I thought of it as a temporal and spatial compromise between two kinds of non-sense: simple repetition and randomized sequence. What appealed to me was the idea of the sentence offering a kind of temporary resistance to the impetus to closure. I wanted to find a way of describing what it is like to enter, move through, and get out of a sentence. From there I considered ways in which stories offer their own kinds of resistance to closure. I was after whatever it is that makes the special rhythm of short fiction, and I wanted a way of explaining how stories compete with other claims on our time. To those who are curious about such things, I offer this book as an extended figure of thought about the art of short fiction.

CHAPTER ONE

Closer to Story

• • •

The protean nature of the literary short story has been eloquently described by H. E. Bates. He says

> the short story can be anything the author decides it shall be; it can be anything from the death of a horse to a young girl's first love affair, from the static sketch without plot to the swiftly moving machine of bold action and climax, from the prose poem, painted rather than written, to the piece of straight reportage in which style, colour, and elaboration have no place, from the piece which catches like a cobweb the light subtle iridescence of emotions that can never be really captured to the solid tale in which all emotion, all action, all reaction is measured, fixed, puttied, glazed, and finished, like a well-built house, with three coats of shining and enduring paint. In the infinite flexibility, indeed, lies the reason why the short story has never been adequately defined.[1]

Whatever the reason, the short story has always eluded any but the most tautological definition; a short story is a story that is short. So it is hard to disagree with Bates's "sensible conclusion that the short story, whether short or long, poetical or reported, plotted or sketched, concrete or cobweb, has an insistent and eternal fluidity that slips through the hands."[2] Pouncing with cupped palm is out of the question. For now, I am interested only in approaches, in ways of getting close. In this chapter I want to remind myself and you of much that has already been said about the nature of short stories.

---

1. Bates, "The Modern Short Story: Retrospect," 73–74.
2. *Ibid.*, 75.

7

The Artless Art

It is generally admitted that the short story, as we know it in the classroom, is a relatively young art form, born of an old, perhaps the very oldest, form of literary expression. Given this genealogy, we might say that the short story came into being when a few people like Poe, Gogol, Turgenev, and de Maupassant learned to polish the manners and tailor the cut of the tale; on the other hand, we might say that story-ing, like dreaming, has always been—and will always be—a very homely part of life. The first way of looking at the form posits an artful art, and it is a view presumed by most of us who "teach" stories. I will return to it in a later section. But the second way is the first I'll explore. It posits an artless art, showing still its folk origins and its popular practice. What are the enduring features of such an ancient art?

In an "International Symposium on the Short Story," published by the *Kenyon Review* in 1968–69, we find hints in a comment like this:

> What is unique about the short story is that we all can tell one, live one, even write one down; that story is steeped in our view and emotion. The passerby who looks up and wonders why one window is lighted in a town at 3:00 in the morning and the invalid looking down who wonders why that woman comes out of the doorway so late, followed by a man more like a jailor than a lover. The short story is what everyone has and so is ever new [and ever old?] and irrepressible.[3]

Here the sine qua non appear to be two: a lifting or bending of the eyes for observation (the simplest, most literal kind of point of view), and a provocation to wonder, caused by some anomaly in the scene. William Saroyan adds another requirement: an audience of listeners:

> [Short stories] *happen* daily to everybody. They are told, with form and style, by the people one to another. This is what happened, this is how it happened, this is why it happened, and so on.
>
> In short, the short story *is*, of itself, central to the human experience; so are the poem, the novel, and the play, but most naturally the short story.
>
> The stand-up comedians of nightclubs and television tell short stories almost without exception. . . .
>
> Is this something like the return of the troubadour, the bard, the singer of the tribal saga? The fact is, he never disappeared.[4]

3. Stead, "International Symposium," 444.
4. Saroyan, "International Symposium," 62.

This feeling that the nature of storying hasn't changed much is shared by Malcolm Cowley. Believing that the form belongs to the common man, he has no patience with those who would deny its common beginnings:

> The present disparagement of story-telling [by certain modern writers] is directed against a very ancient art, perhaps the most ancient of all. [Cavemen told hunting stories, and priests told creation stories.]
>
> *Post hoc, ergo propter hoc* is a logical fallacy, but it is also an essential form of human thought, embodied in the mythology of every culture. A myth might be defined as a doctrine presented in terms of successive events; in other words, as doctrine transformed into story. [But it] is indeed a question which comes first, the doctrine or the story.
>
> I have been talking about the story in very ancient times, but I do not mean to imply that it belongs to the past or will ever become "obsolete."[5]

Now it seems that Cowley, too, is adding to the list of essential features noted by Stead and Saroyan: he wants a doctrine, or a theme—some explanatory or revelatory insight into matters of concern to the tribe of mankind. Have we then got hold of some Ur-model of the story? Is it some raw but malleable life-stuff, a constant of both cave and salon, with rudiments of see-what-I-see, and wonder-with-me, and hear-what-I-say, and think-on-these-things?

The writers I've quoted are reaching after this primal thing by means of general knowledge and passionate intuition. They leave the making of critical theses to men like James Cooper Lawrence. In "A Theory of the Short Story," Lawrence argues that the short story is, indeed, the oldest literary form, predating and forming the nucleus of the ballad and the epic. Furthermore, he says that if we can allow for its originally oral form, the story will have had a continuous existence from the very earliest times right up to the present. So he, too, makes "the story" a monolith. It is coeval and coterminal with the history of man. What appear to be evolutions in form are merely variations in type. Thus,

> For those who insist upon some further subdivision of the great inclusive short story group, it will then be possible to classify short stories in the following manner:
> First, as to substance,
> A — Stories of Fact.
> B — Stories of Fancy.

5. Cowley, "Storytelling's Tarnished Image," 27.

Second, as to form,
A — Stories told *historically*.
B — Stories told *dramatically*.
C — Stories told *didactically*.[6]

Then, as a subheading under "B," he wedges in Poe—and the whole history of the modern short story! *The* modern story is merely *a* kind of story. Yet Lawrence may be guilty, ironically, of a modernist bias, for he claims that the only growth that has taken place in the art of the short story is "a general development in the knowledge of words and the ability to use them" (p. 70). Whatever questions we may have about his theory, we must admit that he shows the important influence of cross-cultural, anthropological studies of literature, studies which are designed to reveal the continuities between "primitive" and "advanced" forms of art. To take just one example, Vladimir Propp's comparative listing of the universally recurrent motifs in fairy tales demonstrates that fiction, especially in one of its smaller and handier forms, can be as primal as love and digestion.

Long and Short Stories

Granting that the story is made of some ancient but ever-young life-stuff, we might become curious about how it is shaped into body, how it looks and does, how it is like and unlike its literary kin. Take a sketch by Hawthorne—say, "Sights from a Steeple." Take a chapter from a novel by—oh, anybody. Take a lyrical prose poem. Each is a brief, imaginative prose-thing. Can't any one of them be called a short story? In his "Review of *Twice-Told Tales*" (1842), Poe says a first and famous "no." He draws a generic distinction. A "sketch" (or, as he calls it here, an "essay" in the manner of Addison and Irving), is *not* a "short story" (or, as he calls it here, a "tale") because it lacks the concentration of all its means to the dramatic end of a "single *effect*." Poe's dicta are too well known to need rehearsing. On their face, his ideas have been accepted and vigorously promoted by other theorists about the form, but increasingly the important distinction has been between the short and the long kinds of fiction.

In 1901, Brander Matthews was blunt. "Now it cannot be said too

6. Lawrence, "A Theory of the Short Story," 63–64.

emphatically that the genuine Short-story abhors the idea of the Novel. It neither can be conceived as part of a Novel, nor can it be elaborated and expanded so as to form a Novel."[7] Following Poe, Matthews sees the essential difference to be the greater unity, or "totality," of the shorter work, but he makes a further distinction that at first seems only amusing: "Another great difference between the Short-story and the Novel lies in the fact that the Novel, nowadays at least, must be a love-tale, while the Short-story need not deal with love at all" (p. 18). The durable phrase here is "need not deal with." Need not—in spite of its forced limitation of scope—need not deal with the whole of life, nor any given part of it; need not finally conform to any expectation—save that of a polished performance. Matthews, really summarizing Poe, tells us that "no one has ever succeeded as a writer of Short-stories who had not ingenuity, originality, and compression; and . . . most . . . had also the touch of fantasy" (p. 23).

If we were to stop and look at what we have now, we might find a very different thing from the cave-fire, mead-hall, and back-stoop yarn. We'd have a precious fellow, a very snob of forms. Must we then assume yet another "essential" trait, or have we come to a genealogical split? When we take the approach by genre, it appears that, despite its folk origins and the above- or below-ground survival of these roots, the art story is a special phenomenon, as different from novels and epics as it is from telephone gossip. For critical purposes, we have a new art form. There are many reasons for its appearance: the expansion of an educated reading public with new but limited leisure, the proliferation of nine-teenth-century magazines with spaces for small-sized fiction, the ro-mantic artist's discovery of the European tale. Some critics would men-tion Gogol's normalizing discovery of the common man as a more compelling subject than primitive marvels. Others would mention Poe's eccentric uncovery of a primitive psyche, a soul-drenching prose. Where to look for guidance? After leaving Matthews, we might very well have to jump sixty years and an ocean. For it seems that the next most impor-tant describer of the short story—as such—is an Irishman.

In 1962 Frank O'Connor (the pseudonym used by Michael O'Dono-van) is still concerned about separating the short story from the novel,

7. Matthews, *Philosophy of the Short-Story*, 26, 18, 23.

but he is also concerned about that hint of preciousness. True stories, he thinks, are more likely to have pathos and grit:

> Always in the short story there is this sense of outlawed figures wandering about the fringes of society. . . . As a result, there is in the short story at its most characteristic something we do not often find in the novel—an intense awareness of human loneliness. . . . The storyteller differs from the novelist in this: he must be much more of a writer, much more of an artist—perhaps I should add . . . more of a dramatist. . . . The novel . . . has a physical body which a purer art like the short story is constantly in danger of losing. . . . It is only too easy for a short-story writer to become a little too much of an artist.[8]

"Too much of an artist? Never!" says Poe. But O'Connor would say Poe is form-proud. Obviously the view O'Connor takes is a mediating one between the two extremes of everybody-can-tell-one and few-can-achieve-one. His is an earnest and valuable, though admittedly a fiercely partisan, attempt to get at the true nature of stories. It may seem narrow in its preoccupation with loneliness as a theme, but perhaps we can free ourselves from the details of his bias and see behind it a large and true insight. What makes the "new" short story different is its flattery of the self as the axis of a world. It may be a small world, a fake world, a tragic or a crazy one; it may be familiar, bizarre, tangible, abstract, reported, or dreamed. It may be but the weirdest fragment, yet it will cast a rounded shadow on our minds. It will revolve on a self. Whose? A single character's often; the author's always; the reader's—but that is speculation for another time. To the list of essentials we will add the one that makes the historical difference: "I"-matters-to-you.

No one gives finer expression to this difference than Elizabeth Bowen. In the same year as O'Connor, she, too, was writing down her perceptions of the short story. Less aggressive than his, not greatly different in substance, they yet carry a finer persuasion.

> The short story is at an advantage over the novel, and can claim its nearer kinship to poetry, because it must be more concentrated, can be more visionary, and is not weighed down (as the novel is bound to be) by facts, explanation, or analysis. I do not mean to say that the short story is by any means exempt from the laws of narrative; it must observe them, but on its

---

8. Michael O'Donovan [O'Connor], *The Lonely Voice: A Study of the Short Story* (Cleveland, 1963), 87, 89, 90.

own terms. . . . I do not feel that the short story can be, or should be, used for the analysis or development of character. The full, full-length portrait is fitter work for the novelist. . . . The short story, as I see it to be, allows for what is crazy about humanity; obstinacies, inordinate heroisms, "immortal longings."[9]

Still trying to divide the story from the novel, Alberto Moravia makes his contribution a few years later. Though he may be more unfair to the novel, he sounds a good deal like Bowen when he says that characters in a short story are individuals, "product[s] of lyrical intuitions," while those in the long form are the embodiments of themes. He, too, argues for the superior artistry of the form. But he takes an even more lenient attitude toward a frank aestheticism: "[The short story is] a literary art form which is unquestionably purer, more essential, more lyrical, more concentrated and more absolute than that of the novel."[10] I think you will see the tendency of these remarks by Bowen and Moravia. There are hints here of a relationship between prose and poetry. So large an issue of genre must be given its due, and in fact as we move closer to contemporary theories of story we will find that these hints become claims. But we're far from through with a consideration of the long and the short of prose fiction. We need to follow genre criticism into the 1970s.

And there we find Norman Friedman. His essay "What Makes a Short Story Short?" is a landmark. It is a rigorous argument for a genre-based, Aristotelian approach to the literary short story, fitting into the larger undertaking of *Form and Meaning in Fiction*.[11] There are definitions here of *intention*, of *plot*, and of *action*. Suffice it to say that an author must start with something to write about—an object of imitation. Plot may be a major or only a very minor part of the "action," which is made up also of character and thought. The author must then decide how he wants the audience to feel towards his characters in their "situations"; in other words, he decides on his end effect, which is to say, his artistic purpose or intention. Having done so, he will then be able to settle questions of technique; if well chosen, his methods will allow him to balance "intelligibility" against "vividness" with the great-

9. Bowen, *After-Thought*, 77–78, 80.
10. Moravia, "The Short Story and the Novel," 152.
11. Norman Friedman, *Form and Meaning in Fiction*, 167–86.

est economy of means. Unfortunately, there is not space to go into Friedman's conception of plot, character, and thought; we can note simply that the overall action and how we are to feel about it predetermines, for the author, certain matters of form. These are 1) what the "parts" of the action will be (*e.g.*, in Joyce's "The Dead," shall Gabriel see his wife dancing with the tenor or listening to his voice?), 2) how the various parts shall be scaled (*e.g.*, shall the dinner-table speech be longer or shorter than the talk with Miss Ivors?), and 3) what their order of presentation will be (*e.g.*, what will be the sequence of Gabriel's memories?). Now these three questions—which parts, on what scale, in what order—have to do with structure and techniques. And, according to Friedman, "structure and techniques . . . rather than style or purpose . . . are primarily determinative of length" (p. 168).

That's the sentence we need to ponder. Friedman says the short story is short not because of its "greater unity," for some novels are as intricately composed as any short story; not because of a static or restricted notion of character—for in this regard some stories are larger than some good novels; and not, finally, because of a limited facility for "culminations rather than . . . developments" (p. 169). These are common explanations for the "shortness" of short stories, yet none of them is adequate. Instead, he has, with surprising directness, averred that the story is short because it deals in short things; its material is of "small compass," and is "cut [down] for the sake of maximizing the artistic effect" (p. 170). Size of action, not kind of action; choice of manner, not choice of intention. These are what make the difference.

Friedman, borrowing from Elder Olson, specifies the kinds of parts —speeches, scenes, and episodes—that make up a narrative. An action of any size may be "whole" (p. 171), and the size will say either "short story!" or "novel!" The smallest action, a speech embodying an immediate reaction to an immediate stimulus, will most likely cry "lyric!" A single scene is usually not enough for a short story, though it's enough for Hemingway in "Hills Like White Elephants." Typically, what we'll find is a single episode. Furthermore, an action-centered theory like this one leads to a distinction between kinds of plots ("mimetic" and "didactic"), as well as kinds of action ("static" and "dynamic"). This second distinction is an important one for the short story:

[A] static story simply shows its protagonist in one state or another and includes only enough to reveal to the reader the cause or causes of which this state is a consequence. . . .

[A] dynamic story brings its protagonist through a succession of two or more states, and thus must include the several causal stages of which these states are the consequence.

Thus a static story will normally be shorter than a dynamic one.

Therefore, although not *all* short stories are static, most static actions are likely to be found in short stories. (pp. 174–75)

Specifying even further, Friedman explains that among dynamic actions there are "simple" ones and "complex" ones. The first have a single line of causation, taking the protagonist from one state of being to the next in a progression; the second have several lines of causation, taking the protagonist through apparently opposite states of being. Lastly, there may be "minor" and "major" actions, depending on how many phases of a life are portrayed.

On discovering Friedman, the short story critic is bound to be pleased. Here is a theorist, grounded at the very source of Western literary criticism, reconceiving, explaining, developing, and applying certain fundamental principles in such a way as to acknowledge and define the authenticity and separateness of the short story genre. Is there, one might wonder, anything more to be said? Surely there is a part of my experience with stories that is well described by his logical categories. Some of my functions, as teacher and critic, are immeasurably helped by his system. I'm willing to guess that I am typical in these respects, that we've indeed found our Aristotle in Friedman. The question that matters is not whether he should or shouldn't be argued with; rather, it is this: are there any parts of our experience with stories that remain unaddressed? For me there are several, and this book is about them.

But let us see what some other critics, also more or less in the Aristotelian mold, can offer us now. A. L. Bader, in "The Structure of the Modern Short Story," argues that the modern story is only *apparently* "plotless, static, fragmentary, amorphous."[12] Seen through a scheme rightly, such stories reveal the traditional elements of conflict, develop-

12. Bader, "The Structure of the Modern Short Story," 107.

ment, and final resolution. The only difference is that the author, working by indirection, takes out many of the connections, leaving to the reader the job of filling them in. Often the author contrives the outcome not as an event but as a "perceived relationship"—a revelation to the reader of the pattern he's been looking for. Bader's notion of "modern" seems conservative now, and perhaps mechanistic: "fill in the missing parts" and get an old-fashioned plot. But he does make us see that some process within the reader can be a clue to the distinctive experience of story reading. How and why, we'd like to know. In "A Critical Approach to the Short Story," Theodore A. Stroud might—but doesn't quite—answer these questions. Like Bader, he wants to rescue the modern story from critical distaste. He'd like to show us that it still answers to the old terms. True, it appears to have degenerated into a mere pretext for "distributing . . . a set of symbols," or into a mere territorial claim, a "'stake' signalizing the fact that some restless genius has explored a new area of the human mind."[13] But in fact the story still responds when asked if it has an end or final cause; it still yields up an "emotional impact," and it still gives us a character undergoing change —or importantly failing to do so. Stroud wants to find a set of neutral structure-revealing questions we can ask of a story, thus avoiding that messier business of describing what *we* think is or should be the "theme." In detailing what to look for, Stroud depends loosely on a theory of "causes," but he's not really a system builder, and, in effect, he lets Friedman write the book.

In passing, now, I should mention one other sort of Aristotelian activity—one that names the species of the genre. "What Is an Initiation Story?" asks Mordecai Marcus. Gregory FitzGerald gives us "The Satiric Short Story: A Definition." And in two pages, Mary Rohrberger offers "The Short Story: A Proposed Definition." Finally! But what she really wants to tell us is that Poe needs refining. He ought to have specified two kinds of stories, the "symbolic" and the "simple," a distinction which roughly parallels the difference between the romance and the novel. It is good to see such beginnings.[14] We might even hope for a

---

13. Stroud, "A Critical Approach to the Short Story," 118.
14. Rohrberger, "The Short Story: A Proposed Definition," 80–82. At the 1980 session of the Modern Language Association, Professor Rohrberger gave a paper which re-

series of such "proposed definitions." Yet we would still not arrive at a theory of the form.

Friedman, Bader, Stroud, Marcus—genre-keepers all. But not everyone is so determined to keep stories and novels apart. We can't end our discussion of genre without recognizing that it is irrelevant to some modern writers. Let me just refer you to Carlo Cassola. He takes a drastic, even a philosophically militant, stand against the idea of subgenres:

> Between the two wars Benedetto Croce's aesthetic theories reigned supreme in Italy. A chief tenet of that aesthetic is the negation of a theory of literary forms or genres. We all shared this opinion, and we were, therefore, convinced that there was no substantial difference between a short story and a novel, and not even between prose and poetry.
>
> I've never had any reason to change my mind about that proposition.[15]

Hans Bender brings the idea fashionably up to date when he explains the practice of new writers in West Germany:

> Their opposition to all existing pre-cast forms, to literary genres and attitudes, includes the short story. Their prose and poetry are presented under the title "Text." "Text" encompasses prose and poetry, and the word points to the indeterminate attitude of the describer, the observer who has not only shaken off the omniscience of earlier writers; from the beginning to the end of his text he maintains his role of the distrustful, doubtful, questioning reporter of reality. He is a spectator, takes notes, succeeds in seeing how things arrange themselves, how something demands to be recognized; but such shreds of observation and memory will never coalesce into an entity.[16]

Bender apparently does see a radical change in the nature of the story, but he goes on to say that he finds the familiar form living on, unrecognized, in particular texts. For "Text" will persist in breaking down into "texts," which will persist in coming from individual writers—who can't seem to help writing stories. Nevertheless, we could think he means to discourage us from looking for the distinguishing marks of the short story; he might want us to think that authors merely dip into the pool of word-genes and come up with a handful of text. If this is so, then criticism of the short story, like homeopathy, is a lost occupation.

---

vealed her continuing interest in, and contribution to, a discussion of the essential traits of short stories.

15. Cassola, "International Symposium," 486.
16. Hans Bender, "International Symposium," 91.

Poetic Fiction and the Poetics of Fiction

Perhaps the largest question of genre—the distinction between prose and poetry—needs to be taken up separately. Indeed, some critics, in writing about story, seem to make it elusive, tender of its author's psyche, wary of its reader's gaze. They seem to imply that the art story behaves like a lyrical poem. At least they like to mention the two genres in what amounts to the same breath. For example:

> [The short story is] as individual as the Lyric itself and as various.
> Brander Matthews (1901)

> [It is] a highly specialized and skillful form, closer to poetry.
> Nadine Gordimer (1968)

> Most modern short-story writers are agreed that their medium is closer to poetry than to a novel.   Thomas A. Gullason (1964)

> The short story is linked with poetry . . . [in that] the susceptibility [to experience] *is* the experience.   Elizabeth Bowen (1936, italics mine)[17]

In each of these cases, "poetry" is invoked as an honorific; the comparisons are meant to enhance the status of short stories. But what is significant here is that each of these writers uses the lyrical poem as a descriptive model for the prose form. The result is an efficient way of saying something about stories. But what? And is it true of all stories, or only of some?

Perhaps the best person to answer these questions is Eileen Baldeshwiler. She has written three articles about what she calls the lyric short story. The first, in 1966 (written under the name Sister M. Jocelyn, O.S.B.), is on "Sherwood Anderson and the Lyric Short Story." There she begins with Paul Rosenfeld's remark that Anderson's stories "really are lyrics with epic characteristics, lyrics narrative of event." She credits him with seeing that "lyricism" may refer to a method as well as to an effect. But it is she who tries to explain what that method entails. I've outlined the stages as follows:

---

17.   The first three quotations are from essays reprinted in May (ed.), *Short Story Theories*: Matthews, "The Philosophy of the Short-Story," 57; Gordimer, "'The Flash of Fireflies,'" 178; Gullason, "The Short Story: An Underrated Art," 19. The last quotation is from Bowen, *After-Thought*, 77.

The writer takes certain "'epic' elements," *e.g.*,
1. "sequential action"
2. "gradually increased intensity"
and manipulates them by using certain "characteristic lyric devices":
1. arrangement of events to emphasize their effect on the perceiver, *e.g.*,
—a "Chinese box" structure of flashbacks, as in Anderson's story "Hands"
—a movement in outer action counterpointed by a movement in inner life, as in "Adventure"
2. "non-realistic, ritualistic dialogue"
3. reader participation in achieving the revelation that is the point of the story
4. "use of symbols to embody and dramatize themes"
5. "exploitation of suggestiveness"
in order to achieve this result: "the poetic short story." [18]

Now in the vocabulary of this system, the significations of "lyrical" and "poetic" are almost the same, and they are no longer vague synonyms for impressionism. Instead, they point to certain specific and observable features of short stories. Taking another important step in 1964, Baldeshwiler generalizes her findings about Anderson and applies them to Katherine Anne Porter. The key paragraph is this one:

> I should like to suggest that the time is ripe for a serious, empirical study of the forms of the short story and that we might undertake this classification by recognizing two basic, recurrent kinds of stories which, for lack of better terms, I shall call the "mimetic" and the "lyric." All stories, of course, have a "mimetic" base, and many, perhaps the majority, achieve their entire effect by presenting in ordinary prose a chronologically straightforward series of events whose significance is contained in and completed by the resolution of the events. Other stories, however, by means of the amalgamation of additional elements into the mimetic base, elements characteristically expected in verse, constitute what I have called a class of "lyric" stories. . . . The "poetic" elements which, in my view, sometimes appear in the prose narrative, include (1) marked deviation from chronological sequence, (2) exploitation of purely verbal resources

18. Baldeshwiler, "Sherwood Anderson and the Lyric Story," 70–73.

such as tone and imagery, (3) a concentration upon increased awareness rather than upon a completed action, and (4) a high degree of suggestiveness, emotional intensity, achieved with a minimum of means.[19]

Some of the differences between this and the previous rendering of her ideas are relatively unimportant—for example, the substitution of "mimetic" for "epic." But other changes show her trying harder to be comprehensive. In Anderson, she noticed a counterpointing of two movements: that of the outward action and that of the inner life. Now she perceives this "cross-grain[ing]" more philosophically as a tension between: "the inexorable outward flow of time which conditions the events and to some extent the quality of experience" vs. "another dominant motif in human existence, man's attempt to isolate certain happenings from the flux of time, to hold them static, to probe their inwardness and grasp their meaning." What she says here is particularly interesting in view of Joseph Frank's theories on the spatialization of form in modern literature. However, she doesn't allude to these ideas directly, but employs them mostly for resonance and as a transition to a more expanded version of another of her earlier points: she argues that the presence of an unfolding consciousness within the story allows the outside reader to "become involved in the integrating process of the central consciousness, sharing [its experience of] probing and discovery" (p. 218). This "qualitative progression" of deepening awareness is "superimposed on the conventional syllogistic form of narrative [and] serves to increase plot unity, to deepen psychological immediacy and to express thematic significance in the 'lyric' story" (pp. 218–19). The counterpointing of subjective and objective, the syncopating of linear progressions, the shaping of the *reader's* experience—any one of these emphases is rich enough to inspire a theory. And in the last of her essays on the subject, Baldeshwiler does attempt, in her words, "a morphology of the genre." Reading "The Lyric Short Story: The Sketch of a History," one is struck by its economy and assurance; it has the marks of a final statement broadening out once again on the basis of earlier research. That her thought is in a mature and balanced form can be seen even in her final decision about the labels to use: "epical" and "lyrical." Her definitions are condensed but telling:

19. Baldeshwiler, "'The Grave' as Lyrical Short Story," 216–17.

The larger group of narratives is marked by external action developed "syllogistically" through characters fabricated mainly to forward plot, culminating in a decisive ending that sometimes affords a universal insight, and expressed in the serviceably inconspicuous language of prose realism. The other segment of stories concentrates on internal changes, moods, and feelings, utilizing a variety of structural patterns depending on the shape of the emotion itself, relies for the most part on the open ending, and is expressed in the condensed, evocative, often figured language of the poem.[20]

The writers who make her "history" are: Turgenev, Chekhov, A. E. Coppard, Katherine Mansfield, D. H. Lawrence, Virginia Woolf, Anderson, Conrad Aiken, Katherine Anne Porter, Eudora Welty, and John Updike. She would like to see them studied as exemplars of their kind. Perhaps that is a worthy task for criticism, although it will be noted that what she calls the "lyrical" features of these writers have, for the most part, been appreciated in other studies of their work.

One can't say, either, that she changes the short story canon. As Charles May points out, neither has she added to our knowledge of the kinds of short stories; we knew they could be "poetic" before—though we couldn't have said so well why. Finally, she herself has commented on the tendency of such terms as "lyrical" to devolve into similes.[21] Yet if there's room for reservations, they only prove how eagerly and hopefully these articles have been read, how far forward they stand in how scanty a field, how much we want a comprehensiveness they only start to provide. "The Sketch of a History" is valuable in itself and as a prototype, and I'm inclined to think that Baldeshwiler has done more than anyone in recent years to establish a "field" of short story criticism. She has done the groundwork for those who will come along with a more specialized vocabulary for story effects, for distinguishing between the "poetry *in* fiction" (or, how fiction borrows from poetry) and the "poetry *of* fiction" (or, how fiction makes prose into art).

So now let us look at the critics for whom the lyrical poem is only a disjunctive analogue for the short story. They say that the characteristics of the poem merely alert us to qualities in fiction which must then be explained through a special understanding of how prose, not poetry,

---

20. Baldeshwiler, "The Lyric Short Story: The Sketch of a History," 202.
21. In a letter to me, dated June 28, 1976.

works. It seems we can't have everything at once, for the first person who may be helpful to us here is talking about what stories are said to abhor—the novel.

In his book *The Lyric Novel* (1963), Ralph Freedman tries to do more than compare fiction to poetry; according to him, "lyrical fiction . . . is not defined essentially by a poetic style or purple prose. . . . Rather, a lyrical novel assumes a unique form which transcends the causal and temporal movement of narrative within the framework of fiction. It is a hybrid genre that uses the novel to approach the *function* of a poem" (emphasis mine).[22] He wants us to notice those strategies of address, those ploys of connection that govern an author's choice of a medium. Explaining further, he says, "Essentially, what distinguishes lyrical from non-lyrical writing is a different concept of *objectivity*. . . . The lyrical novel, by contrast [with novels of man and world interacting in time], seeks to combine man and world in a strangely inward, yet aesthetically objective, form. . . . The lyrical novel absorbs action altogether and re-fashions it as a pattern of imagery" (pp. 1–2). Now, if we remember that the "new" short story seemed to be the result of 1) more sophisticated techniques for unifying the presentation of material, and 2) greater concentration on the role of self, then we can see that Freedman's "strangely inward, yet aesthetically objective, form" is the result of 1 and 2, in business together. In order to follow his argument we'll have to bring to mind again Joseph Frank's article, "The Spatialization of Form in Modern Literature." There we learn how poetry, in particular, but also some kinds of prose, can work by an additive principle of accreted imagery. The words will yield their meaning only at that moment when the design as a whole is perceived. Frank's point is that the conventions of print force us to read sequentially, by clumps of threads, while the meaning of what we read may lie in the handkerchief-text as a whole. Usually, this overall spatial design is created through patterns of imagery. Their "progression" may have a linear dimension of change or modulation from point X to point Y, but the integrated figure is as important as the way it evolves. Some critics stress the static shape of the final design; others stress what Baldeshwiler called "the pattern of qualitative progression." Freedman does not go much beyond her when he

22. Freedman, *The Lyric Novel*, 1.

speaks of the "surge toward greater intensity" (p. 8). If only he could explain how that "surge" is transmitted! But he is conceptually so tied to the modular unit of "the image" that he is less interested in other phenomena beneath the too-familiar visibilities of scene, event, character—and image. It will be a contention of mine that the short story is a better place than the novel to look for, watch, and describe such phenomena.

Beverly Gross is an example of a critic who has learned Frank by heart, who has a well-trained eye for the ever-present "image," but who also has a commitment to the intrinsic features—and beauties—of prose.[23] She's being properly sensitive when she makes a distinction between "poetical" fiction (which uses devices of poetry like alliteration, "rhythmic reinforcement of meaning," etc.) and "poetic" fiction (in which the experience of the story is inseparable from what is done to its language). Another truism, to be sure, but she pins it down neatly. Says she, the experience of Katherine Anne Porter's "Flowering Judas" is the experience of participating in re-vision, of being one with a passionate intelligence expressing itself in a distinctive blending of irony and pathos. This experience is formed, as the language is formed, by a qualifying appraisal of Laura's commitment to illusion. And how, specifically, is the language put together? According to Gross, it is repeatedly made into sentences that depend on coordinating conjunctions; these, in effect, are pivots upon which opening clauses of "simple statement" turn into "elaborating [ones of] counterstatement." Illusion; disillusion. That is the pattern of the language, and, therefore, the substance of the experience. At once, we might want to ask, "But how do Laura's, the author's, and our experiences differ—yet coexist?" And mightn't syntactic features be only one of several sentence-level phenomena we need to examine? My answer would be that the second question could lead us deeper into the first one. The point is, we need a way of breaking through the once-helpful but now limiting analogy between lyrical poetry and poetic short fiction.

To see where the analogy has taken us, consider Howard Moss's anthology of short stories written by poets. In his introduction Moss seems to be saying that the technical differences between poetry and fic-

23. Gross, "The Poetic Narrative," 129–39.

tion are less important than certain other differences in ways of looking at the world. While it might be true that poets traditionally look into mirrors while fiction makers look out of windows, it is more wonderful to note that some imaginative people are "mirror-writers," while others tend to be "window-writers," and that prose and/or poetry may come from them both.[24] As he tries to show in his collection of stories by poets, a short story may very well express a poetic sensibility. But the end result of all this urging may simply be to sharpen our interest in just exactly what it is that makes the poet turn just now, just here, to prose—and prose that happens to look like short fiction. For I am not so much interested in why stories behave like poems. At the present time, the more important question seems to be this: when, how, and why does prose behave like a story?

Languages of Short Story Criticism

"Figures of Life"

And now would anybody want to say that fiction is indeed not poetry, because fiction doesn't really know yet what it is—having cribbed from other genres all its life—but that if it is like anything, it is like music? William H. Gass might say something like that. At least he's always willing to say that fiction isn't a way of getting at truth. Writers aren't specialists in knowing whatever it is they're writing about. No. "What writers know is language and how to fiddle [with it]."[25] Gass claims that this is "just the symbolist position, really." In his case, however, it is generated by philosophic rather than aesthetic propositions. For him, both philosophies and fictions are conceptual systems; as such, each obeys the laws which govern its making; hence, no system can pretend to any truth but internal consistency. Yet some philosophies, some fictions, are more important than others. Why? Well, because they form more telling models—not imitations, not transcriptions, but independent models—of something we want to know more about. Life. The philosophic models are related to daily experience as the Pythagorean theorem is related to the distance between the top of a steeple and the tip of its shadow on the ground. Fictional models, on the other hand,

24. Moss (ed.), *The Poet's Story*, xiv.
25. Gass, "A Symposium on Fiction," 4.

are related to daily human experience as the word *rose* is related to the word *love* in "my love is a rose." Now one of the differences among fictional models is a difference in the quantity of inference needed to make the significance tell. When a great deal of inferring is required, we are probably reading a poem; when the construction is very fully elaborated, we may be reading a novel. In between we'll find the short story, or, if the conceptions are more philosophical than fictional, perhaps a critical essay—like those collected in Gass's book *Fiction and the Figures of Life*. These essays are all gorgeous displays of word fiddling. Trying to pick them over to help make our own case seems a little like unraveling a tapestry in order to patch up a quilt. But let us say that what Gass contributes to our survey is 1) a passionate advocacy of short fiction's "completeness," 2) a critical assumption that the efficacy of fiction is not in its "life-likeness"—either in the ease by which we can visualize what is presented (often hardly possible in the very best fiction), or in the ease with which we can recognize the characters as "real" (which they can't be and shouldn't be), but rather its value is its imaginative suggestion and immediate beauty as a thing made out of the sensual and conceptual properties of words; hence, 3) a methodological shift away from a criticism of language as a vehicle or medium through which ideas are conveyed (by devices often described by analogy with poetic techniques) toward a criticism of language as the conceptual material out of which things of little art or of great art are made.

Criticism of the short story needs, of course, to know more. It needs a way of talking about language phenomena that doesn't require subordinating fiction to the practice and values of poetry, *nor* indenturing it to a philosophy that assumes a Cartesian void between the sign and its referent. Story criticism also needs a better way of describing what gives totality to the work of fiction. We want to know what it is that gives the period to the clause, that ends the "fiddling" at some point. Is it mere exhaustion of desire? I write, Gass has said, in about forty-page breaths. Has every writer a breath-span, or does every genre have one? We need, too, a way of explaining the reader's experience in terms that do not make him either a passive captive or a co-creator. Reading Gass, we are spellbound, caught in the harmonies of syntactic rhythm, the descants of diction. He is a very Pan of prose, but he has very little to say about why some melodies are short stories, while others are not. In William

Gass the art of fiction has a formidably intelligent, a ruthlessly imaginative advocate. Yet, in a way, all he tells us is that words are but words, and that stories are made of them.[26]

Formalism

Gass's conclusion may be a tease, but for the short story critic, it is a given. The question is, how basic can we get? Well, perhaps we can start with this: every known language provides its users with a way of designating an "X" to be talked about and a way of doing the talking, of associating with "X" all the things one might say about it. That is, every language provides for the acts of denomination and description. If so, wouldn't such a universal occurrence of the means for doing these things suggest, then, the universal presence of the faculty, desire, even the need for doing them? Tzvetan Todorov reminds his readers of George Boas' conclusion: that universal "grammatical concepts" argue the existence of universal "psychological processes."[27] This is not the place to debate whether experience takes the shape of the mental categories used to perceive it, or whether these categories come into being as the most efficient means of coping with the environment. Either way, one could still argue that the adult reader has learned to comprehend the world by the sentence-ful, even as he has learned to breathe by the lung-ful. Todorov's poetics of fiction, which incorporate and extend work by Victor Shklovsky on the sentence and story, starts with the assumption that fiction is a conscious manipulation of the universal processes underlying the very structure of language itself.

What we get is a grammar of fiction. In fact, of course, stories exist as conglomerates of sentences, but it is possible to see this total sequence as a large-scale sentence composed of many small ones. Thus the story would be related to the sentence as an embroidered x across a pillow is related to the thousands of cross-stitches making the pattern. What "makes" story can then be expressed in terms of what "makes" sentences. "We shall understand narrative better," said Todorov, "if we know that character is a noun, the action a verb" (p. 119).

Remembering those elementary acts of naming and describing, we

---

26. A fuller treatment of Gass's views appears in Chapter Two and Chapter Seven herein.

27. Todorov, *The Poetics of Fiction*, 109.

realize that they depend on the primary perceptual categories of same-
ness and difference. Without established continuities, we could use a
word only once; without the recognition of difference, we could use
only one word. By match and mismatch we extend the boundaries of
what we can label, what we can predicate. This is our way of coming to
"know." Todorov steps from this elementary truth about how the mind
works to an elementary truth about how narrative is conceived. In a
sense, the way we get from a statement to a narrative is the way we got
from a tautology to a meaningful statement: "Narrative is constituted in
the tension of two formal categories, difference and resemblance; the
exclusive presence of one of them brings us into a type of discourse
which is not narrative" (p. 233). By anticipating some of my own work, I
could illustrate Todorov's point in the following way: we need to get
from a series of resemblances ("He came. He came. He came.") to
something short of a series of meaningless differences ("He came. He
didn't come. He came.").[28] Todorov's suggestion? "Transformation represents precisely a synthesis of differences and resemblance, it links two
facts without their being able to be identified" (p. 233). In other words,
we must get to plot ("He came. He discovered. He suffered.") by
"transforming" our simple sentence "He came."

In a chapter called "Narrative Transformations," Todorov brings to
the story-sentence the insights which transformational grammar has
brought to the sentence itself. To use his own example, we might begin
with the kernel "X commits a crime," and then work upon it one of the
simple transformations of "mode," "intention," "result," "manner," "aspect," or "status." Here is what we would come up with:

X must commit a crime.
X plans to commit a crime.
X succeeds in committing a crime.
X is eager to commit a crime.
X is beginning to commit a crime.
X does not commit a crime. (pp. 226–27)

There are also more complex transformations, such as that of
"appearance":

X pretends that X is committing a crime. (p. 228)

28. See Chapter Five, the section entitled, "Story as Rhythm: Periodicity."

Do you feel in the presence of plot? Perhaps all we have so far is the makings of plot. Something is missing, and Todorov tries to supply it through notions of "equilibrium" and "disequilibrium." He says that story "subjects" are described (by story "adjectives") to be in a state of either equilibrium or disequilibrium; story "verbs" are what describe a passage from one of these states to another. Thus, "the minimal complete plot consists in the passage from one equilibrium to another" (p. III). More complex plots involve transitions from a state of equilibrium, through a state of disequilibrium, to a state of new equilibrium. It is hard to disagree. But, as they are used here, these terms simply point us back to life, to a grammar of experience in which, for example, a happy marriage is an equilibrium, a divorce a disequilibrium, and a remarriage a new equilibrium.

Following this approach to story has stretches of glide and sudden deadends. It is exhilarating to feel that at last the anatomy of story is within our reach—to feel, in moving from Aristotle to Todorov, that we have moved from the naked eye to the microscope. But a slice of tissue is not the body we love, nor even its little finger. It is merely essential knowledge. For my own part, saying that the sentence is the universal integer of experience leads to much that I would like to say about story. And it seems to me worthwhile to pursue the notion of equilibrium within the framework and the nature of story itself. So, as you will see, the work discussed here has had a major influence on the view of story developed in the rest of this book.

Organicism

Once again we are back to the holistic idea of story as something always other than and in a sense simpler than whatever ganglia of words or sentences may constitute its being. Let's look at some critics who conceive not so much of an artless art as a natural art, a life-saving art. William Carlos Williams is a good example. Analysis is just what he won't do. He'll not take his forms by design. He'd rather let his work create its own shape. Yet, in an article on "William Carlos Williams and the Modern Short Story," J. E. Slate makes us see that Williams is hardly an "automatic" writer. He believes in careful notation. If not case histories, then case stories, case poems. It's the skill of keeping up with the symptoms, of meeting the shocks. Improvisation should be con-

stant and canny—a method not of ducking but of catching the blow
where it's aimed. Says Slate, more academically: "Techniques [of im-
provisation] may be improved by closer imitation of the violence and
deformity of our daily life, constantly reinventing forms nearer and
nearer to the truth about us."[29] I am calling Williams an anti-formalist,
though perhaps I could call him a de-formitist. Pattern, design—these
may well be, but life speaks more aggressively in the mutating fact than
in the normal assumption. The itemized, formal features of any genre
become its expectations—which are the things we may have had before
we made house calls. Afterwards, we'd have known better. We'd have
seen life laboring to be born as phenomena. Never quiet, always
squirming.

For Williams, life may always have been recalcitrant; for Nadine Gordimer, it seems to have become so, and, in the process, to have lost
whatever neatness and comprehensibility it may once have had; it is
now so fragmented, so incoherent and inconsistent, that no two observations can maintain a fixed relation to each other. The short story, because of its brevity and concentration, is the most usable form left to
literature. In it, only "a moment of truth is aimed at—not *the* moment
of truth, because the short story doesn't deal in cumulatives."[30] It deals,
instead, with "the flash of fireflies." For Gordimer, a new, more co-
hesively interdependent society might generate a fiction of sustained
life. On the other hand, Williams, like many doctors, might guess that
the end of one disease is the starting of another. But both these artists
view the short story as the survival form of fiction. It can shape itself to
the particles of reality without unduly falsifying them or losing its own
entirety.

Another critic who finds reality often a disintegrating image is Elizabeth Bowen. Cinema, she might say, has helped us to see a universal
flickering more disruptive than the come-go of the sun. But more than
almost anyone I've mentioned so far, she has a literate sense of the formal evolution of the story. Her introduction to *The Faber Book of Modern Short Stories* is an extraordinarily intelligent and well-written piece.
There she reviews the history of the form, citing de Maupassant and
Chekhov as the initiators of the two major (and contrary) influences on

29. Slate, "William Carlos Williams and the Modern Short Story," 658.
30. Gordimer, "'The Flash of Fireflies,'" 180.

the English short story. According to her, the Frenchman displays "astringency, [and] iron relevance," while the Russian favors a "romantic distension." The contrasts continue: "simple, lurid themes" vs. "a system of irritations beautified," a hard "impersonality" vs. "a cloudy detachment, charged with pity." While de Maupassant taught both Irish and American authors, Chekhov helped form Katherine Mansfield. Bowen is tough-minded in her criticism of writers who mistake Chekhov's casual ambience as mere self-indulgence. But she is no advocate of cold technique. Having earned her critical wisdom, she spends it in a clear and lovely testament. The story, she says, has a "necessariness"; its germ is "a vital fortuity" fed by "amazement." Every good story must have a "valid central emotion [which is] austere, major," and yet it must also have the "inner spontaneity of the lyric."[31] Fictions do not revolve in orbits determined by relative mass. Neither do they take dictation from phenomena. Stories grow. They come into being within the deepest recesses of the nourishing spirit. It is Eudora Welty who says simply, "A story becomes."

More explicitly and centrally than Bowen, Welty is an organicist. For herself she forswears analysis, yet her essay "The Reading and Writing of Short Stories" is an argument fully and firmly articulated. It is particularly interesting because it deals with both the writing and reading of stories; the two acts define a reciprocal relationship based on the giving and receiving of pleasure. Writing a story is a private function, a concentration of energy, but it is powered by the desire to please others, who will then cry for "More!" Writing may be a lonely act, but it leads to a social exchange—warm, civil, supportive, yet purely anonymous. Instinctively, it seems, her criticism guards her privacy while answering to the reader's interest in the author. The creation of a story, she explains, is governed by the arrow of time, renamed the arrow of creation; that is, conception and execution represent a forward movement, an evolution through stages of being. As reader-critics, we falsify both the process and the result if we try to break a story into parts that can be disassembled and recombined. Form isn't plotable. "It is the residue, the thrown-off shape, of the very act of writing."[32] Since the author didn't "put it together," the critic shouldn't "take it apart." Well, maybe

31. Bowen, "The Faber Book of Modern Short Stories," 153–54.
32. Welty, "The Reading and Writing of Short Stories," 171.

not. Welty makes it seem ungracious—and insensitive—to argue. She cajoles us into feeling we ought to be her kind of reader-enjoyer. "A story behaves, it goes through motions" which leave traces, felt as form. Or, to follow her changing metaphor, we feel the "atmosphere" of each story, its "mystery of allurement."

There are many kinds of atmosphere. Playing critic, Welty names a few of them. For example, there is the "atmosphere of action," which can, as in some of Hemingway, be acrid with emotion—fear, let's say. There can also be the "atmosphere of sensation," as in D. H. Lawrence, or of "intellectual sensuousness," as in Virginia Woolf. What is remarkable here is not so much her terminology as her receptivity, her exquisite understanding of what each author sends her, and her ability to write the most eloquent of literary thank-you notes. Yet again, we shouldn't miss her broader insights. "On some level," she says, "all stories are stories of search . . . [and] corresponding to the search involved is always the other side of the coin" (p. 170). Apparently her arrow of time has a momentum. The push and pull, the sway of desire, has a way of making the see-saw into a trajectory. In a remarkable phrase, she tells us that the source of beauty is "the quondam obstruction." It's because Hemingway can't get around his fear that his stories are a way to get through it. It's because Faulkner can't keep space and time within bounds that his prose finds a way to unloose them. Reading Welty on the reading and writing of stories is to feel that one has been made politely at home with a marvel. We learn how to wonder efficiently. She teaches us to look at the complementariness of the reader and writer and to guess how it works. Don't we feel her getting at a rhythm? Author filling reader till he tips—with all he's heard. Reader tipping author till he spills—with more to say. But what are we sensing our way toward?

The logical culmination of an organic view of story is simply to see the story as an organism. That is just about what Randall Jarrell does in his introduction to *The Anchor Book of Stories*.[33] I have been saving this essay. Perhaps I've even ordered my survey so as to end with Jarrell— though I might just as well have begun with him. For he is a believer in the ancient gods—and ancient life—of story. An antigeneric critic, he'd

33. Jarrell, "Stories," 43–44.

find stories in dreams, in poems, in letters, in gossip. They grow every-where, in cultivated or uncultivated minds, and they grow out of seeds-of-story, out of some often tiny or surprising reminder of the conflict between the pleasure and reality principles. Oh, yes, Freud is at hand. He supplies many of Jarrell's terms, helping him to dramatize the psyche of the writer. Dream-wishes heave into being, shoved by desire, only to be met by reason's "no," society's "no-no," reality's "never." Anywhere along this psychic route a story may be born. There are sto-ries of fantasy doomed by fact, of fantasy claimed as fact, or of fantasy indifferent to fact.

Whatever the kind of story, there is a narrative which brings the reader along without his knowing he's been taken. It's a linear move-ment, Welty's arrow of creation, but the final story has not so much a route as a life-span. The end, however, isn't just the last word. It is the finality of surcease—for the story, and for our involvement as readers. Like the limit of a breath held under water, our interest builds and bursts; or, like the deeper sigh that interrupts calm breathing, our ac-quiescence ends. Some stories give us an experience of "continually in-creased excitation"; others bring us back to a state of repose. Intuitively, Jarrell has made fiction one of the life functions. Metaphorically ellip-tically, he's brought us to the very edge of a new start, a new way of looking at stories.

How far, then, have we come? We've seen the origins of story in that ancient and ongoing human activity—tale-telling. We can never escape the matrix of tale, teller, and told. But we've seen Poe and others declare the independence of the art story, not only from oral traditions but from novel and poem. For a very long time, no one added much to what Poe had said about the specialization of technique in the short story form. Later critics would point out resemblances to the lyric, the romance—but such comparisons would lead to emphases on symbol-ism and imagery in general. With New Critical methods, scholars could do analyses of theme, structure, and tone in story after story after story.

As we've seen, genre-wide criticism doesn't get a good start until *The Lonely Voice*, and technical theorizing really begins with Friedman, Bal-deshwiler, and the Formalists. For an introduction to the scattered rich-ness of what has been offered in the way of commentary on short fic-tion, there is no more valuable source than Charles E. May's collection of essays, *Short Story Theories*. Many of the critics I've been reviewing are included there, and May's bibliography, wide-ranging and helpfully annotated, is a further guide to academic, literary, and journalistic discussions of the genre. My own survey, though fairly representative, is far from exhaustive.[34] Clearly I've been guided by my own interests, and so, for example, have given much more attention than May does to rhetorical, stylistic, and structuralist approaches to fiction—whether or not the authors thought they were talking about story poetics. From all these sources—from May's book and from a wide variety of theorists on language and narrative—much can be learned. Those who have tried to get at the sentence-level workings of narrative, those who have tried to conceive of a generically unique reading experience, those who have tried to escape vocabularies derived from the study of other genres, and those who have tried to put their hands on that elusive thing, the life of a story—these are the people who seem to me to have the most to contribute to a genuine aesthetics of short fiction. Their influence is everywhere in the pages that follow.

34. The spring, 1982 issue of *Modern Fiction Studies* is entirely devoted to articles on "The Modern Short Story." These essays have much to contribute, and I regret that I was unable to discuss them before sending this book to press.

CHAPTER TWO

Sentencing the Story

• • •

Starting to speak of stories, we begin with that end-stopped thing—
the sentence. And I could, by way of initiating my argument, say that
the sentence unit is more important to the short story than to either the
most discursive poem or the most poetic novel. Poems have periods,
but they come by the line, in the space, on a breath. Reading a poem,
we enter a retracted language—re-taken, re-made, re-tendered—in
which syntactic norms are not wholly to be trusted. Novels, of course,
are usually sequences of sentences, but also of chapters and parts. Reading a novel, we enter a protracted language, or series of languages, in
which syntactic norms (however eccentric in relation to "ordinary" use)
must be taken for granted. In short, a poem seeks, by its nature, to sub-
vert a prose continuum; a novel, just as naturally, depends on creating
one—no matter how faceted or internally varied. What, then, does a
short story do?

Reading a short story, we enter a contracted language, in which syntax is the very structure of understanding. We do not always get a simple economy—Mark Twain proved that sentences may ramble toward
pointedness—but always a delivery in full. By the sentence-ful. As we
know, others have argued that the sentence unit is in some ways a paradigm for the story unit, and although that is not exactly my claim, I do
find it possible to identify on the sentence level certain features of the
composing and of the reading processes that are typical of, and prominent in, the experiences we have on the story level. Naturally, I do not
deny the value of studying the sentences of a novel, nor do I presume
that any given sentence could, for any intrinsic reason, be more at home
in a story than in a novel. But I do mean that we pay attention to sen-

tences in stories because we have to, because if we dally over the
nuances of a word, if we skim for the drift, either way we are missing
literally the sentience of the story. We are missing the experience of
being acclimated to the story-world, of assimilating all that it interposes
between the beginning and the closure we want—and yet don't want—
to reach. The nature of that experience, the very essence of the art story,
is the subject of this book. To appreciate it we must get closer to sentences as sentences than we customarily do when reading either poems
or novels. I hope to persuade you that you cannot really talk about stories without first learning—in detail—how to talk about sentences.

"Signs" of Fictionality

For a start, come with me to a point before fiction. Consider the sentence as the smallest unit of meaning in prose discourse, and ask your-
self whether it can be identified as fiction. I hear you say, "Naturally
not." But let me suggest that we could look for certain signs in a given
sentence which would lead us toward story. The first might be the "intentional" sign, by which I mean our recognition of what Roman Ingarden calls the "intentional correlate" of the sentence, its direction of
reference—whether it be toward a real "state of affairs" that exists independently of the sentence, or toward a "*purely* intentional state of affairs," which exists only as a postulate of the sentence itself.[1] Take, for
example, this sentence: "Mary was at the library all afternoon." If we
grant priority (and validity) to the referential function of the language
here, we might say that we have a statement of fact; the sentence corresponds to an objective state of affairs that, first of all, exists whether or
not the sentence comes into being, and, second, can be verified by the
laws of that objective realm. Since corroborative empirical evidence is
one of the ways of establishing "truth" in this realm, we might find it
relevant that Peter actually saw Mary at the library, and that Nancy
heard her voice.

But suppose Mary wasn't really at the library at all, but went instead
to the movies. And suppose that her sister, wishing to cover for her, tells
their suspicious mother that "Mary was at the library all afternoon."
The sentences are identical, but their "intentional correlates" are not.

1. Ingarden, *The Literary Work of Art*, 128–44.

The first sentence points to an objectively "real" situation, while the second points to a "purely intentional" one. Yet the second is masquerading as the first, and is therefore a lie. But of course to make that identification, we need to know more than the sentence alone can tell us. In isolation, it is potentially both kinds of sentences. It is also potentially a third kind. If we happen to know that Mary is a character in a story, then the sentence is a "fiction" because Mary is. She is purely intentional (existing only as that to which the word points), and so all that is predicated of her must be so, too.

But what about a sentence like: "The cat was robed in her dignity, but condescended to wink 'hello.'" Does figurative language, in itself, change the ontological status of the sentence? After all, the cat is not really wearing a robe, nor is dignity a garment, nor do winks speak English. It would seem that the sentence correlate is purely intentional. But quite possibly the creator of this sentence wishes to convey something "true." Not an objective fact, perhaps, but maybe a subjective one? To me, the cat "really and truly looks as though. . . ." So, for our purposes, this sentence may be classed with the one about Mary; both are potentially true, although true to different kinds of realities beyond themselves. Or they are false. To those same realities. We would need to apply an "intentional" test, and we could do so only if we had more knowledge than the sentence provides.

Sometimes, however, a sentence can be made to say "I'm fiction" right away. Let's call this the "semiotic" test. It depends on our recognizing that a given sequence of words contains clues that, in our shared understanding of the language, means "something not real." For example: "The unicorn bowed, and the poodle replied, 'I'm so pleased to meet you.'" There's something we want to say for the poodle that we didn't have to say for the cat. We want to say that the poodle can't be real. Here let me slip again into Ingarden to say that the sentence is obviously pointing to an unreal or imaginary world, though one that is "intersubjective" (*i.e.*, recognizable to many people). The dominant semantic feature of "unicorn," for our purposes, is its ontological status as imaginary. Thus, there is a nominative key to the status of the sentence—its subject names a fairy tale creature. Since the poodle is syntactically linked with the unicorn, it partakes of that animal's status. So strong is this imperative that it changes the intention of poodle; a dog which could be perfectly "real" in another country of the mind, here has to be as imaginary as the unicorn. But we have a verbal key, too. The poodle "said." Poodles don't "say." The difference between a cat winking "hello" and a poodle saying "I'm so pleased to meet you" is the difference between a potential figurative truth and a potential imaginary truth. In this case, both are more or less intersubjective, since most people are accustomed to the personification of animals and the idea of a unicorn.

Other sorts of commonly recognized keys are possible, too. Indeed, conventions of story telling have created certain "modifier" keys. Who wouldn't guess he's into fiction when he reads: "Once upon a time there was a king who had two ugly daughters." The obvious tag here is the first four words, but I'd also contend that something happens to "ugly" —because it is under syntactic pressure to belong to the world of that opening phrase. Our familiarity with fairy tale superlatives, with drastic transformations and simple dichotomies, makes us expect either that "ugly" will turn into "beautiful" or that "ugly" will signify "wicked." But here we're on the verge of something we might fashionably call "the grammar of expectation."

First, however, let's look at another test that is more of a presumption than a detection of "fictionality"—and that is the "literary/aesthetic" test. It does not establish the ontological status of the sentence, but it notifies us that there has been at least a partial transfer of importance away from the simply referential function of the words and toward the kind of pointer the sentence is. When this happens, we usually expect that the character of the pointer will tell us something about the character of what it's pointing to. That is, when we descry, or even merely sense, that the sentence creator has invested a great deal of care and art in the formation of the sentence, we are on the alert. And we usually find that art is conspiring not so much to inform us about some X in the real world as to make us realize the kind of world that could have this X in it. When we feel the shift, we begin to feel in the presence of fiction.[2]

2. See Gass, *The World Within the Word*, especially the essay entitled, "The Ontology of the Sentence." I share with Gass the disposition to view literary language as contextually conditioned to a degree and in a way that ordinary, transactional language almost never is. At first it might seem that Gass's fictional construct exists in the same plane as Ingarden's intentional correlate. However, Ingarden's notion is phenomenological (locating events of consciousness on different levels of abstraction); Gass's notion, despite its

Another step, and I shall be into "affective stylistics." My debt to In-garden will explain why much of what follows sounds like the kind of "reader response" criticism developed by Wolfgang Iser. But most of all, I must acknowledge the influence of Stanley Fish, whose work became known to me after I had written the early drafts of this chapter. I am grateful to him for confirming my belief in the value of close attentive-ness to the behavior of sentences. Obviously, I feel that his kind of "in-formed reading" is at the heart of appreciating the art story.

The Story of a Sentence

Let me now give you a sentence that can be helpful to us throughout this discussion. It is from Nadine Gordimer's short story, "The Train From Rhodesia," and goes as follows: "The flushed and perspiring west cast a reflection, faint, without heat, upon the station, upon the tin shed marked 'Goods,' upon the walled kraal, upon the grey tin house of the stationmaster and upon the sand, that lapped all around, from sky to sky, cast little rhythmical cups of shadow, so that the sand became the sea, and closed over the children's black feet softly and without im-print."[3] Taken in isolation, the sentence would seem to be a statement of combined objective and figurative truths. Potentially, it could have the status of intending a real state of affairs. Certainly there are no semi-otic clues that the sentence intends an imaginary world. Indeed, there might very well be a railroad station in Rhodesia which could be recog-nized from this verbal description, and there could have been a moment of time in which the details recorded here did, in fact, exist, and would have done so whether the sentence ever got written or not. On the other hand, it is quite possible that we would have to visit several sta-tions and observe many trains arriving before we could—but you see what I mean. The sentence *might* refer to a reality—taking therefore just a little slide on the scale from nonfiction to something else.

Pushing the obvious a bit further, we could conceive of the greater

---

philosophical vocabulary, is essentially rhetorical (engaging the reader in a transfer of be-lief from one master context to another). My analyses of sentences are somewhat similar to Gass's. However, I have proceeded by slightly different steps and toward a different end. I have tried to clarify the difference between "figurative truth" and "imaginary truth," and to establish the foundation for a discussion of constraints, rhythm, and closure in the short story.

3. Gordimer, "The Train from Rhodesia," 43.

difficulty of "verification" if the sentence creator had remembered the cupped shadows from an experience having nothing at all to do with railroad stations, and furthermore (and more fancifully), if we were able to track down the shadows—but didn't see them as cup shaped. For many readers, even the knowledge of where the sentence comes from will confirm only that it was written for the purposes of a larger fiction (the story) and apparently contains some references both to objective reality and Gordimer images. These images can, of course, be analyzed into their referential components. But to say that "cups" refers to (or names) an object that we could also describe as a hand-held, semi-spherical container (and, by the semantic transformation we call meton-omy, as that which such a container contains)—and to say that certain shadows share semantic features with (and may therefore be meta-phorically denoted as) a cup or that which is cupped—all this is to give our attention to features of the sentence that are irrelevant to the fiction reader. It is only when we see "cups of shadow" as mediating between author and reader, as creating an image beyond the sum of its referential parts, that we begin to assess the literary function of the sentence. It is only when we realize that that image belongs more to a world we don't yet fully grasp than to a world (that of real Rhodesian railroad stations) that we may know about from other sources—it is only then that we feel the quickening of story. To put the case another way, we have evi-dence that a possible metonomy and a positive metaphor have occurred. But whether these "events" are described phenomenologically (as the Gordimer subject and the world object interacting to produce a ver-balized datum of consciousness) or linguistically (as the semantic disso-nance created by selecting "cups" from among possible substitutions for the head word in "something of shadow"), in either case their value in the sentence can be judged only if we know we have fiction. If we don't know that, we have only the "literary" test to guide us. In this case, it would prejudice our guess in the right direction.

Now, in my discussion so far, I have overleapt the author to sit with the reader. Naturally. For the author (presumably) knows whether or not he's writing fiction, and at the moment we're interested in the signs which tell the reader it's fiction. But can we get beyond the signs we've already mentioned—and very superficial ones they are—without get-ting beyond our view of the sentence as a fused and finished thing? Can we much longer overlook the fact that a sentence is an entity that *comes into being*? Granted, the process may seem instantaneous; granted, it is always unrepeatable and untraceable—even by the author; and granted, no reader in the process of reading a story wants to relive the birth of a sentence. But I am going to hope that we can aid our quest as critics by letting ourselves play author. Temporarily. Hypothetically. For let us say that innumerable constraints, in shifting waves of interaction with purpose, bring a sentence into being. No one, not even the maker of the sentence, can do more than guess at what has happened. Yet we will look at some guesses. I'm going to try to illustrate what I mean by a "dynamic of constraints," even though I can't reconstruct the actual dynamic of any sentence—not one of my own, and certainly not one of Gordimer's. We must also remember that any list of constraints I may posit are ones which I can adduce from the sentence in isolation, whereas by far the most important constraints will be those which are imposed by the requirements of the story as a whole. But if these two provisos can be kept firmly in mind . . .

Let our author want a Rhodesian station, and let her first constraint be verisimilitude. We will imagine her asking herself, "What words will signify what can really be seen, felt, heard, experienced of this station?" Perhaps she can visualize many such stations or only one in particular. It hardly matters, for other constraints inevitably and complexly interfere. Some of them may come from the real world within which the station independently exists; so, for example, sun dictates shadow. Others come from the nature of the verbal medium itself; so, for example, it may be that the prevalence of [k] sounds (in "sky to sky" and "cast"), of [ə]'s and [p]'s (in the series of "upon's" and "lapped"), as well as the many [s]'s ("sand," "sky," "sea," "softly") suggests to the inner ear "[k]+[ə]+[p]+[s]"—"cups"—of shadow, rather than flaps or waves of shadow—even though, semantically, these other choices may harmonize as well or even better with "cast" on one side and "sea" on the other. Or again, it is possible that the length of "rhythmical" is felt as a subtle pressure for some shorter word than "depressions" or "declivities." Just as easily, the force of suggestion may emanate from the sand-as-sea image, the idea starting out simple enough, but working back through the veins of the prose to demand a container for that watery shadow. A cup. Clearly, too, the tide of meaning can flow the other way, making the sea an after-thought of the cup. Of course I've only hinted, and very hypothetically, at the interplay of semantic, syntactic, phonetic, and rhythmic influences that, in infinitely varied and modulated ways, leave a word on the page. It's worth noting, too, that even if verisimilitude played a minor part in the choice of "cups," once the word was on the page, it could come to fully and exquisitely signify to the author what she had actually seen. Why, those shadows *do* look like cups! Semantic serendipity. Without it, what story could come into being? With it, what authorial joy!

Yet after all, we're only intruders on this joy. I've played at entry into the writer's mind for one purpose only: to suggest that if we believe the sentence in fiction comes into being through the interplay of constraints, then we may be able to find different but related terms for describing that sentence's effect on the reader. We may be able to go beyond what we have so far been able to say about the "literary/aesthetic" test for fictionality. So let us now forsake author playing and return to one reader's response.

The old questions come up first. If there is a sense in which the author is his own first reader, is there a sense in which each reader creates his own text? A phenomenological view would insist on the difference between the body of words identified by a given title (or even any sentence or word of the text) and the reader's "concretizations" of the symbols on the page. To the extent that no two speakers of the same language have had exactly the same experience with any word in its lexicon, and to the extent that the grouping of these words into syntactic units ramifies and complicates their relation to the reader's linguistic and experiential frames of reference, patterns of association, etc.—to these incalculable extents, any given sentence will be "read" differently each time, and hence authored anew.

Another old question is whether the reader's experience of the words imitates the author's appreciation of their meaning. Is the reader transposed into the author's mind, or, to put the more limited question that is traditionally asked, does the reader visualize what the author (or his character) sees; does the reader experience to a greater or lesser degree (depending on the "success" of the work) a cognitive and/or affective echo of what he would "know" or "feel" were he actually undergoing the named experience? The notion that fiction provides *this* kind of surrogate reality, a field for vicarious experience, is now presumed to be outdated, or is so meticulously qualified that it is hardly worth mentioning. William Gass, for one, denies that the fiction writer is giving the reader cues for mentally reliving some "real life" experience.[4] The best fiction, in his opinion, does not help us to visualize anything "out there." It does not, for instance, project the picture of a landscape on our brains; rather, it gives our eye the direct experience of a wordscape. I would guess, therefore, that Gass would urge us not to close our eyes and try to picture "cups of shadow." Rather, he would have us see that phrase in its relation to the final topography of the accreting words. If we "visualized" anything, it might be the subliminally realized shape of the sentence, felt first as it comes into being with its lapping repetitions, its ebb and flow, felt finally as it has become, when its movement is seen as the course it has taken. Thus the sentence is immediately apprehended as a sensuous object and as a conceptual design rather than as a window on life. That design may be (and will be if the writing is excellent) congruent in many points with (i.e., will be a metaphor for) the author's perception of what is important and true about a station in Rhodesia.

I believe that Gass is eloquently right about the ontology of sentences. But we still need a way of talking about the experience of reading them in fiction.

The Impetus to Closure

Our first job is to account for the physical "body" of the sentence as well as its function as a specific order of verbal signs. It seems hardly necessary to bring up again the fact that a written English sentence exists in both space and time. For now, let's concentrate on what that means for the reader: he undergoes a sequential process which is yearning toward a static result; he is experiencing an impetus toward closure, blocked by various kinds of interference which are in one way and another removed, surmounted, absorbed. It's important to realize that "interferences" is hardly a pejorative term here. I'm referring simply to whatever the words do to us when we read rather than skip over them. One might similarly say that the respiratory system "interferes" with breathing.

4. See "The Concept of Character in Fiction" and other essays in Gass, *Fiction and the Figures of Life*.

Filling a blank space between a capital letter and a period does indeed slow the path of our eye from one to the other, but it certainly makes the path more interesting. Yet we always want to get to the end. Where this "impetus to closure" comes from is a question for another kind of study, but I think we can assume that what the linguists call "competence in English" (putatively possessed by all native speakers) includes the internalized expectation of the period, just as it includes the rules for generating sentences that *do* end. It will be necessary, however, to explain what I mean by several kinds of closure. These are:

Physical closure: achieved simply by reading to the end of the sentence. It may occur almost automatically, or may involve turning a page, taking up the words again after some unexpected interruption, or even getting to the end after pausing over a word or backtracking to link up a phrase.

Cognitive closure: achieved by arriving at an understanding of what has been read. It may be further specified in two kinds:

Immediate: achieved when we grasp the surface meaning of the words, apparent to anyone who can read English (yet still not exactly the same for all readers).

Deferred: achieved when we arrive at an understanding of the full significance of these words in this story. It can never really be reached, especially in a story that provokes serious thought. Nevertheless, it can be used, in argument, to point to stages in the appreciation of residual meaning.

And now I would like to categorize those aspects of the sentence which interfere with or complicate this achievement of closure. I'm going to use the terms *density* and *intensity*, and will take them up in order.

Linguists will, I hope, forgive me for using some of their vocabulary without all of their knowledge. I do not, as I have already shown, believe that a creative writer begins with a "kernel" sentence within which he systematically "embeds" units of information (or "propositions") by means of a series of "transformations." Naming these mechanical processes only gives us a convenient way of denoting the features of the final product, which may have come into being as organically as a child or a cancer. It's easy enough to see the difference between "He didn't say anything" and "Knowing he was being watched by the other men at the counter, he didn't say anything that would have compromised him, but he felt all the more irritably ashamed of her."[5] Of the many ways to describe the difference, one would be to say that the second sentence is the product of a greater number of transformations—for example, the modal verb and relative clause transformations which allow the noun phrase "[it] compromises him" to be embedded into the sentence "He didn't say anything," with the result we have seen. Francis Christensen uses the term *dense* to describe sentences with a high quotient of embedded information—and particularly of added free modifiers—and the term *thin* to refer to those with a lower quotient.[6] A child learning to read would naturally feel that a "dense" sentence was harder to get through, or longer in the getting through, than a "thin" one. Mature readers can usually read both with almost equal ease, but reading a prose of mostly thin sentences will still be a different experience from reading a prose of mostly dense sentences. The kinds of interference to closure will be different. For inherently, the dense sentence is no more involving than the thin one. It simply involves us in a different way.

Having briefly considered syntax, we must start over again—with diction. Now surely a word's effect is partly a function of its syntactic placement, but, since we are temporarily in the business of separating the inseparable, let's put syntax aside and focus our attention on words. Can we, for example, define a semantic something or other which we can call "intensity"? And might not some of the "intensity" be intersubjective (to use, again, Ingarden's term)—*i.e.*, felt by all who speak the language? For example, aren't there functional words like *said*, and aren't there affectively more "loaded" words like *moaned*? Can we begin by saying that some words carry stronger affects than some others? Then perhaps one sort of "intensity" has to do with the kind or degree of affective stimulus a word conveys ordinarily or in a particular context. We must, of course, realize that the emotional power of any given sentence or even phrase is hardly to be explained as the summed affect of the individual words, and we must also admit that an apparently neu-

5. Adaptations of a sentence ["He didn't say anything."] in Raymond Carver, "They're Not Your Husband," 21.

6. Christensen, *Notes Toward a New Rhetoric*, Chap. 1, *et passim*.

tral sentence like "He didn't say anything" could have more affective weight than "He murdered his wife." What matters is the context.

And if we can be stimulated affectively, can't we also be stimulated in other ways, too? Whatever requires "figuring out," whatever requires us to call upon the myriad schemes of knowledge we possess, whatever engages our question-raising, problem-solving interests—these might be called intellectual stimulants. Here, as with affective stimulants, it is dangerous to concentrate too long on single words in isolation. I start with them only because, occasionally, a single word *can* hold up a sentence, or, more usually, a kind of word can do so. For example, here is the opening sentence of a well-known short story: "The mental features discoursed of as the analytical, are, in themselves, but little susceptible of analysis."[7] We might be beginning a treatise—and a dated one—on the faculties of reason! The prose is stiffened by the nominalization of adjectives and verbs, by the high level of abstraction, and by the frequency of words associated with argumentation. What exactly are "mental features," we wonder, and what does "analytical" mean here? Though we've temporarily separated diction from syntax, it would be unreasonable not to appreciate how the syntax reinforces and emphasizes the effect of key words: by withholding crucial information, placing it late in the syntactic order, the author not only highlights certain nouns but also engages us in a participatory act of reasoning. He states a near contradiction which, when perceived, needles our minds. As you might guess, we are in the hands of Poe. He wants us in the hands of Dupin. He wants us ready for a "tale of ratiocination" ("Murders in the Rue Morgue") in which the slayings of two women will serve primarily as a catalyst to thought. Passion *is* here, but it is the ecstasy of pursuing and arriving at solutions to puzzles.

Now all of this discussion of "interferences" has posited qualities which are more or less intersubjective, which might be said to be "there" for anyone sharing the author's language and cultural context. But surely the effects of "density" would vary with each reader's skill at following cues for grouping words, and each reader's sensitivity to rhythmic patterns such as final cadences.[8] Even more obviously the

7. Poe, "The Murders in the Rue Morgue," 146.
8. Patrick (ed.), *Style, Rhetoric, and Rhythm.*

effects of "intensity" would vary with each reader's experience. Each of you has already had an opportunity to read the Gordimer sentence, and will be able to compare your experience with mine. Her sentence is both "thick" enough (as the diagram below shows) and "intense" enough (as I will now try to demonstrate) to give us a good example of a sentence that richly interferes with the impetus to closure.

We have here an almost textbook example of one of Christensen's cumulative sentences; it is syntactically "dense," though not complexly so:

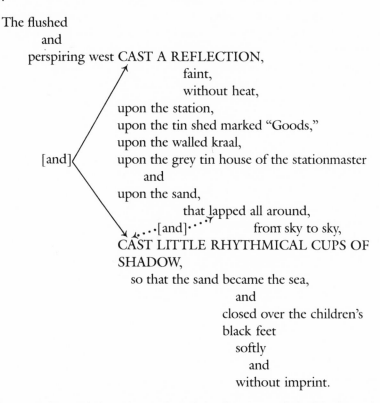

The second "cast," though an echo of the first, is parallel with "lapped." And look at "closed." It's part of the series of verbs telling us what the sand did: lapped, cast, and closed. But were it not for that comma after "sea," "closed" would be parallel with "became." Then those feet would be covered not by the sand which is merely wavelike, but by the sand-which-is-now-the-sea. In this sentence there are grammatical pairings but there are also mirages of parallelism that mean something, too. The perspiring west *is* partly responsible for those shadows, and the first sand is and is not the same as the "sea" that erases the "imprint." We're left with a vague sense of interrelation, rather than a clear impression of causality.

Intensity, or the relative specificity or vividness of the "concretizations" we achieve, is a more nebulous feature. But let me admit that I have never imagined the western sky as an overheated face. "Kraal" is in no lexicon of mine. And I have no idea whether the word "Goods" was painted in white or black, above or beside the door (if there was one), in five-inch or in two-foot-high letters. And though I have seen many reflections cast, though I know what some tin objects look like, though I am familiar with sand and sea, and though I have seen many black children, still, the mental effort of even very imperfectly "visualizing" the total scene described here would be a separate and subsequent act of mind; it did not occur as I read the sentence. Now, I would go so far as to agree with Gass that fictional prose has an ontologically separate and richly apprehendable body, and that readers are primarily engaged in the act of knowing that body. But I would not agree that this knowing is limited to an appreciation of lexical, syntactic, or even rhetorical phenomena—unless one stretches those terms like letters on a blown-up balloon. For there is an evocation, a calling forth, by the sentence, of something which I experience as I read, something other than a mental picture of the "scene."

I find here that Ingarden's notion of "spots of indeterminacy" is very helpful—if inverted. He points out that the potential stock of meanings belonging to any word (and, by complication, to any phrase, etc.) will yield an actual stock of meaning determined by the context *and* by the reader's predilections. Furthermore, since the full complement of aspects belonging to any object which might be described could never be exhausted by a verbal description, the necessity for choice in any prose (and for art in any fiction) yields a "schematized" rendering of the aspects belonging to the object represented. Thus, we have "black feet," rather than the still hugely incomplete but more fully determined, "five-to-six-inch human feet of a gray-black color fading at the instep." Ingarden suggests that various readers fill in, in various ways, few or many of the "holes," the "spots of *in*determinacy." Now, in reading the Gordimer sentence, I feel no compulsion to determine the size and color of the letters forming "Goods." On the other hand, I do feel a compelling interest in the children's feet that only vaguely requires that there be, or that I see, bodies and faces. Perhaps it is relevant that I have myself, in the past, not only seen feet drowned in sand, but have felt the almost liquid grittiness of very dry sand laving the tops of my feet. And is that relevance made manifest by some sympathetic correlation of my mind's eye with Gordimer's, some "identification" that enriches and validates the experience of fiction? I would have to say no. I am not filling in "spots of indeterminacy." Rather, I am responding to what is especially determined, concentrations of affective and intellectual stimuli, crests of intensity, which are determined partly by my susceptibilities, but largely by the author's management of the sentence. Positional emphasis certainly has something to do with the power, for me, of those cupped shadows and buried feet. Syntax conspires to throw attention on the direct object of the repeated (yet delayed) verb "cast"; in addition, lexis has been tampered with to generate figurative duties for "cup," making this word more intensely meaningful than it usually is in "cup of coffee." Thus, spots of determinacy occur when 1) the lexical and syntactic patterns focus the emphases of density and intensity, and 2) there exists in the reader a resource of affective susceptibilities that may never be verbalized, and a residue of cognitive habits that have subsided into a pool of likelihoods, of preferred ways of "taking the sense" of things. Having "got to the end" of the Gordimer sentence, we achieve physical closure. Having "taken its sense," we achieve cognitive closure. But—and here is the essential point—we may feel that in some sort of way this closure is not final.

If we step back from our sentence, forget, for a moment, our intimacy with its parts, deny to it the special privilege of our study, make it stand up for itself as an ordinary sentence—what, after all, does it tell us? What are the actions and who or what are doing them? A reflection is being cast upon a series of surfaces presented by the environs of a (Rhodesian) railroad station; in particular, the sand is casting shadows, and finally, the sand is becoming the sea and is closing over some feet. Yet there's something oddly oblique about this information. Shed, house, station, sand are all under the influence of—not a light source, but its reflection. Indeed, the reflection is being cast by a word that literally has nothing to do with light sources, that means only a compass orientation opposite to east, and that is further disguised by an impressionistic figure of speech (though a perspiring face *may* glisten and so reflect light). "West" only becomes endowed with the power to shed light by its syntactic position as the subject of "cast," and by its connotative association with the setting sun. And how does sand become sea? Only by the operation of an association within the mind of the viewer. And where and who is the viewer? That, of course, is the question. The nominative and verbal elements of this sentence are so completely subordinated to the modifier elements—to information about how things appear—that the sentence as a whole functions primarily as a modifier, a scene setter, an attitude conditioner. It leaves us with an unresolved question. To whom does this scene look this way? For whom can the dust become water? For whom is the unifying light capable of subordinating and equating the buildings and transforming the sand? The art of the sentence has withheld the answer only to make it more pressing. And finally, I think it is fair to say that our desire to know "who," to enrich and personalize the point of view, is a desire already beginning to fulfill itself. The sentence is itself evidence of a sensitive observer, a perhaps wistful and certainly imaginative one, a viewer for whom the values in what is seen are given by the very act of appreciative attention to what is uniquely offered. If I am describing too exactly the young "heroine" of the story, it may be the fault of my having read beyond the one sentence. But I would argue that the sentence by itself carries both realized potencies and a suggestion of complements. It satisfies the impetus to closure, but at the same time it contains forces of anticlosure. Now, the same might be said for any sentence; each plays its part in initiating, as well as completing, a grammar of expectation. But the sentence that says "I'm fiction" raises questions that are not the kind an essay could answer. Reading the Gordimer sentence, we do not feel compelled to ask for a treatise on railroad stations. Indeed, the degree to which we want an explanation of the kraal is the degree to which our appreciation of the story, as story, is hindered. But probably we wonder a little more noticeably about what the black children are doing there. Most of all, though, we want to know what sort of world a "flushed and perspiring west" belongs to—a world, that is, in which sand can lap feet. It's the world we need the story to show us, for it exists nowhere else. That world is the "story correlate," just as the total sense of a sentence is the "sentence correlate."

The Sentence in a Story

It's time now to return to the supposition that the sentence, as a unit, plays an especially important role in short fiction. Many have claimed that the short story is the most end-conscious of literary forms. Though there is much to be said about the reasons for this assumption, we may safely say now that the story binds its reader less closely to the word than a poem does, and more closely to the sentence than a novel does. (The exceptions which come to mind, such as Joyce's *A Portrait of the Artist*, are novels that in many ways move deliberately closer to poetic language, and therefore pass through, or exist in, something like the short story's field of force.) Though I've been arguing that a sentence *may* predispose us to regard it as fiction, it would be impossible to re-fine the identification further, to say "this sentence belongs to a short story rather than to a novel."

And yet the fact that the end is pushed closer in a short story does impart a really quite practical urgency, a quite necessary efficiency, to each sentence that takes up time, that both delays and brings closer the terminal point. The short story sentence is thus under peculiar obliga-tions. What I have been calling the features of density and intensity may be found in any sentence; however, in artful short fiction, they are more likely to be significantly controlled, manifoldly determined, and tensely composed of elements that defer narrative closure while allowing both physical and immediate cognitive closure. The anticlosure elements will point us always toward a fuller rendering of a story correlate in which humanly interesting agents do, are, or become (or not) something in such and such a way (or non-way) in such and such a place (or non-place). Naturally, the presence and function of the anticlosure elements will depend on the position of the sentence in the story; earlier sen-tences will be richer in anticlosure than concluding ones. Longer ones may seem more fictional than short ones, though of course they aren't. Our earlier example, "He didn't say anything," is certainly "thin" in terms of density, but its intensity can hardly be underestimated when we read it in a story by Raymond Carver. Even in isolation, its emphasis on the nominative and verbal elements makes us wonder about the modifiers—about all that is withheld about this kind of "he" and his world.

Yet even where the urge to read on is strongest, the resistance encountered by the reader, in the truly artful sentence, has a shape that makes the achievement of immediate closure a peculiarly unified experience. That experience can become the basis for defining a kind of rhythm and may, in turn, help us to understand what happens in the story as a whole. But in this chapter, we have concentrated our gaze on the sentence. We have seen how it may bear some of the marks of fiction, and I have suggested that these signs are more likely to be present in the sentence of a fiction that must hasten to an end.

CHAPTER THREE

Getting into Story

• • •

Where—and when—do we begin to have story? Had we better look for it *between* two sentences? Does it appear only after we sense a design? Can we say that we "have" it until we've read to the end? This is the first of three chapters which will explore these questions, and I will try to start at the beginning.

The Ontological Gap

In one sense, a story is surrounded by a moat, an ontological gap between itself and the "real" world. I'm of course speaking now of what might be called the "story correlate"[1] rather than of the pages and sounds that do, in fact, exist empirically. From this point of view, there is no negotiating across the barrier; one is either in or out of the world of the fiction. And yet, for the reader, the physical embodiment must be reckoned with to a degree that presumes only one avenue of approach—through the "beginning." For a moment, then, let's look at that point which is both a serial datum of the "real" world ("page one," "word one") and the initial datum of the "fictional" world. As we found when examining the intentional nature of the individual sentence, we often need help in distinguishing between discourse that points to a reality independent of the pointer, and discourse that intends merely what it postulates. In practice, we find such help in the fact that collections of stories are usually labeled as such, and individual ones appearing in magazines are often subtitled "a story." Later, perhaps, we will be able

---

1. By analogy with Roman Ingarden's "sentence correlate," which signifies the meaning of the whole generated by the disposition of marks on the page, but existing on a different ontological level from those marks.

to dispense with such cues—but for now, let's give ourselves their benefit. Knowing, then, that we are starting a story, what can we say of that
start?

For a very philosophical meditation on the nature of beginnings, we
might turn to Edward Said. His book *Beginnings: Intention and Method*
is a remarkably personal, eclectic, and suggestive treatise on what it
means to "begin." Much of his concern is with the problems of initiating critical discourse, but some of his more general speculations are
relevant here. They read like sententia:

> To have begun means . . . to have initiated a course discontinuous with
> other courses.
>
> Words . . . *are* the beginning, of a series of substitutions. Words signify a
> movement away from and around the fragment of reality [which they are
> "about"].
>
> To use words is to substitute them for something else—call it reality, his-
> torical truth, or a kernel of actuality. . . . The difficulty of this method is
> that it does not imitate nature, but rather displaces it.[2]

His point about the nonimitative function of language, a view shared
by Gass, is familiar by now. What is interesting is the emphasis on a
radical discontinuity between reality and language, or, to put it more
conveniently, between two kinds of reality: the kind that is not mediated by language (what we experience in the act of sitting down and
opening a book, or even in the movement of eye muscles, the register-
ing of visual cues that allow us to distinguish between "cat" and "bat")
and the kind that *is* mediated by language (what we experience as we
start the act of reading in a meaningful sense). There is a gap, a kind of
ontological moat, between these two orders of experience. We must
cross this gap. We must get adjusted to what lies on the other side of it.
The world of the story.

The opening words, which may often be those of the title, will be our
first information about that new world. We are on the alert, aware of
the immanence of the story correlate which it is the business of each
new sentence to support. But of course we don't yet have possession of
what only the story as a whole can give to us. We may find ourselves
very easily achieving both physical and immediate cognitive closure

2. Said, *Beginnings*, 32, 65, 66.

(*i.e.*, getting through and to the "point" of each sentence individually), and yet feeling very much in the dark. We read those opening sentences as we may assume Adam would have read Genesis: it is new information and we cannot get enough of it because it is all we have to tell us where we are and what matters there.

In my discussion of the sentence, I suggested that some sentences, though grammatically complete themselves, seem richer in "nominal" information (having to do with subjects that *do* or *are* something), while some are more potently "verbal" (telling us about an action or a state of being), and others work more generally as "modifiers" (setting the scene, conditioning an attitude, etc.). Our presumption, which may eventually be sharply reformed, is that we are working toward a complete "sentence"—a fulfilled grammar. That is, we look forward to a story correlate in which humanly interesting agents do, are, or become (or not) something in such and such a place (or non-place). What I have elsewhere called the anticlosure elements in the sentence are those which arise out of our sense of the imbalance or incompleteness in our concurrently growing, altered, confirmed, shaken, constantly reformulated sense of the whole. Thus the first sentence is, no matter how obvious in its referential function, almost totally composed of anticlosure elements; one could almost say that however clear its sentence meaning, its story meaning is opaque. And hence the initial experience of a story, the encounter with its beginning, occasions in the reader a necessary loss of at-homeness. Some fiction writers try very hard to disguise this fact, while others boldly exploit it. But the fact remains that a lag of understanding exists.

Bridging the Gap

"Reaching across, he said, 'Here it is.'" You're puzzled. "Who's 'he'?" you ask. And "Where's he reaching?" and "What's he got?" and "Who's he talking to?" The implied object of "across" and the pronouns "he" and "it" are examples of what Joseph Backus calls "sequence signals." Normally they are words which refer back to information given earlier in the discourse. A page ago we learned that her boyfriend went into the war, carrying her silver locket, promising to keep it safe, and now he's sitting in the kitchen, saying "See?" and reaching across the old table: "Here it is." Or we learn that he's hunched against the tile in the men's room, having paid in cash, and the man he's seen only once before reaches over a barrel of soiled paper towels, handing him the packet and saying, "Here it is." Two different stories. Two different kinds of stories. But suppose there are no prior pages? Well, then we have a temporarily obscure reference—an abuse of the language system, but a vivid illusion of being catapulted into a story's world. This is the effect Backus is describing in his article "'He Came Into Her Line of Vision Walking Backward': Non-sequential Sequence-Signals in Short Story Openings."[3]

He charts the types and frequencies of common sequence signals (like pronouns) and draws some modest conclusions about the historical development of story beginnings. The earlier authors tend to recognize the discontinuity factor and to compensate for it by supplying transitional exposition. For example, a writer like Hawthorne will sometimes undertake our initiation outright, as in the well-known stories "My Kinsman, Major Molineux" and "Roger Malvin's Burial." Both stories begin with expository passages that ease the reader from his own time and place into the historical milieu of early New England. Naturally these opening passages perform other functions as well. But by overtly accepting the reader as a visitor in his fiction, and by courteously guiding that reader through the vestibule of story, Hawthorne is, in part, following the decorum of an older form—the genial "sketch." On the other hand, modern authors often try to hide the gap. Some even give a stylistic feint of continuity. In many Hemingway stories, for example, there's a presumption that we already know the he or they referred to in that very first sentence. The author wants to make us believe that the world of the story is not just contiguous with the one we're sitting in, but also in its essence identical with life "as it really is." Backus' statistical data underwrite his thoroughness (he reviewed 1,001 stories!) and give him a large margin of safety in drawing conclusions. These inferences turn out to be only more narrowly defined versions of truisms about the historical shifts in literary style from the nineteenth to early twentieth centuries. But they offer concrete evidence of the ontological gap between the reader's reality and the story's. Not only centuries but authors, too, differ in their ways of bridging—or widening—the gap.

3. Backus, "'He Came Into Her Line of Vision . . . ,'" 67–83.

Reality Warp

It may be philosophically accurate to say that we are in fiction's world the moment we cease to be engaged with our own—when we submit, that is, to the very first word. Experientially, however, we may find ourselves undergoing a transition which deepens, conditions, and builds upon that initial fact of entry. In teaching the short story to undergraduates, I have often found it wiser to underplay the ontological separateness of the story's world and to delay any talk of verbal constructs and story correlates. Instead, I've urged my students to regard the story as a phase within the reality of their daily lives, a phase distinguished by its demands for a more consistently high level of attentiveness, a phase intensified and magnetized by the pressures of significance until it bends back on itself, perhaps many times, to become a "reality warp." Though the analogy with "time warp" is admittedly very loose and faddish, it does lead to a more serious thought: the possibility that the story, while both an "ontically independent sphere" and a separate physical unit, is also a phase of our lives which must be entered with help. If, for the moment, we may be cajoled by the idea of a "reality warp," we may consider that our entry, still beginning at "word one," continues through a period of reorientation.[4]

How long are we at the beginning? More often than not, for at least a paragraph—but there are some stories that make the whole notion of beginning seem putative—and there are others which have pages of frank introduction. Perhaps the best rule of thumb is to say that we are past the beginning once we know what's at stake and for whom. But for the sake of emphasis and detail, I am going to use an even more truncated form of beginning. Below are the first one or two sentences of three well-known short stories:

> Whoever has made a voyage up the Hudson must remember the Kaatskill mountains. They are a dismembered branch of the great Appalachian family, and are seen away to the west of the river swelling up to a noble height and lording it over the surrounding country.[5]

*

4. This progressive "familiarization" of the reader with the specific world of the story is not really at odds with, and actually complements, Victor Shklovsky's notion of art as a "defamiliarization" of the real world.

5. Irving, "Rip Van Winkle," 29.

None of them knew the color of the sky. Their eyes glanced level, and were
fastened upon the waves that swept toward them.[6]

*

Braggioni sits heaped upon the edge of a straight-backed chair much too
small for him, and sings to Laura in a furry, mournful voice. Laura has
begun to find reasons for avoiding her own house until the latest possible
moment, for Braggioni is there almost every night.[7]

For reasons which will become clearer in the next chapter, I am going
to discuss the first two examples together, followed by a separate discussion of the third.

Here to There

Do you remember what you were doing just before you sat down to
read these stories for the first time? Even if you were relaxing on a Hudson River cruiser or fighting for survival in a lifeboat, even if you could
come impossibly close to making your life lead into the world of the
story, still you would notice the ontological gap. Put less philosophically, you would have to sit down. Or lie down. Or, at the very least,
grab a handhold on the subway. You might think you have to stop your
own life to enter the story's—but in fact, you are simply entering a
phase of your life called "reading a story."

Irving's first sentence may or may not seem to welcome you in. The
sentence subject here is a nominative clause, which in turn has an indefi-
nite pronoun as subject. Not "you remember" or "I remember," not
even "they"—but "whoever has made a voyage up the Hudson." This is
a category of people especially favored, but only as a group and only
because they must remember the Kaatskills. Maybe you have never even
been in New York State, but you are now a candidate for nostalgia by
proxy. The sentence predicates—making a voyage up the Hudson and
remembering the Kaatskills—are far more salient features than the
strangely vague subject. But "whoever" will expand to include "you," as
the opening paragraphs take us on just such a voyage up the river.

"They" begins the next sentence, and refers, of course, to the Kaatskills. "They" even belong to a family, exhibit nobility, "lord it over" the

6. Crane, "The Open Boat," 68.
7. Porter, "Flowering Judas," 90.

countryside. Is this a story about a family of mountains? That initial premise will be modified as the "voyage" takes us further up the river and deeper into the past, until at last we meet a fellow named Rip. Still, there are more than a few good arguments for keeping those lordly and timeless mountains as the subject of the story's sentence. By the time we meet Rip, we're in a world that defines its human characters in relation to landscape and timescape, and does so in a certain way. To describe that way is to describe Irving's imaginative creation, to point to the story correlate, or, finally, to define the reality warp.

But may I now toss you into the roiling waves? No leisurely cruise, but a desperate drift? "No one of them . . ." Of whom? A perfect example of a "nonsequential sequence signal"! "They" exist already. They've been out there in that open boat all the time we've been finishing up the ironing, putting the kids to bed, doing whatever we have to do to free ourselves for a book. How many of them? What do they know? What are they doing? With superb reductiveness, Crane gives us "no one of them," tells us what they *didn't* know, gives us "color" without a color, and names only "the sky." Here there is no genial, inclusive "whoever," but a harsh, exclusive "them." This experience is *theirs*. As information, we get the barest minimum of setting, of condition of being. Each little bit more that we get will be grabbed. Bit by bit. "Their eyes glanced level" (staring? hopeless? hypnotized?) "and were fastened upon the waves" (ah! sky and waves, sea and sky . . . no land?) "that swept toward them" (aren't they moving? can't they make progress? can't they make waves of their own?). Irving, remember, is kind enough to take us gradually back to a far point in time, from which his story can move forward. But Crane puts us dangerously close to four shipwrecked men and points them and us toward a speck on the shore.

Here to HERE

We may feel the leap into "Flowering Judas" primarily as a shift into a more demanding attentiveness. The first sentence goes to work not so much through ellipsis, indirection, or reduction of information—and consequent arousal of curiosity—as through a replete and highly determined delivery of meaning. In the terms I used for explaining sentence closure, this sentence offers a relatively high degree of interference; it is both syntactically dense (though not unusually so) and semantically in-

tense. It tells us a very great deal. Its grammar is largely fulfilled. Braggioni and Laura, Laura and Braggioni. Can we imagine that they are *not*
the characters the story's about?

Braggioni. Braggadoccio. Laura. Laurel. The vaunting god of the
lyre. The tree that was the nymph who fled all lovers, even him. Where
are they now? In a room. In a house. Does town, country, or century
matter? It's more important, initially, that the chair is small and straight-
backed, that it's the kind of chair Laura has in her house, that Braggioni's unfit for it. But if we know something about who and in what
circumstances, do we have any idea about what's going on? Braggioni
sits heaped. Braggioni sings in a furry, mournful voice. He is there almost every night. Laura has begun to find reasons. Oddly enough, the
present tense doesn't seem to bring us into physical proximity, as we
might be if we read "Braggioni is sitting heaped upon the chair, and is
singing to Laura." There we'd be, and we might wonder just what he
was singing. But the "sits" and "sings" are, in this story, a custom. The
"has begun to find" is a new development, already underway, more an
arrived state of mind than a decision we witness. Things have happened—or refused to happen—but what we feel is the salient bulk of
Braggioni, a thereness so oppressive it keeps Laura from going home to
her own house.

The part of the grammar that's missing is the "because"—Laura, "because she was a certain kind of person," avoided Braggioni. "Because. . . ." Because anyone who sits "heaped" in a chair too small for
him, and whose singing voice is "furry," is bound to displease someone
who has "straight-backed" chairs and "reasons" for repulsions? Of
course it is absurd to say that these sentences tell us of Braggioni's fatu-
ousness and Laura's compulsions. But I don't think it is absurd to say
that Porter's opening prepares us for a different story than, say, either of
these two openings:

> Braggioni sits balanced in his chair, singing to Laura in a throaty and
> mournful voice. Laura has started coming home later, knowing he'll
> be there, disturbed by the feeling he gives her.

> Braggioni rests his fat on her chair, singing in a furry voice he likes to
> call "mournful." Laura has begun to think of her house as his rutting
> grounds, and hates to go back there.

The tone of each example is different, but both are blatant and relatively uninteresting—unless you're looking for standard romance or comic relief. Porter's tone, as Beverly Gross has pointed out, is stringently but subtly ironic; it reaches us through the "loadedness" of the modifiers, which let us guess much more than the characters know. It works through the doubly and trebly determined signals of each noun, verb, and phrase. It works by holding us up and loading us down—by interfering with closure in such a way that we possess more information than we know we have, hints that require a spreading and deepening elaboration. They are clues that will eventually make sense not as markers on a linear path, but as parts of a puzzle that is Laura. When we finish, we may not know quite where we've gotten until we think back over and into and around where we've been.

I see that I've brought myself to the point of speaking as much of endings as of beginnings. And of course the way an author helps us "get into story" has a lot to do with the way he wants us to "get out of" it. But whether we feel launched on some trajectory, or placed on the edge of a carpet, the beginning of a story is the point of greatest ontological shock. Afterwards, we are in an increasingly better position for getting our bearings in the story.

CHAPTER FOUR

Getting Through Story

• • •

The first sentences of a story—no matter how closely interlinked—are really more consecutive than sequential. From the reader's point of view, the number of acceptable second sentences may be so great as to be effectively infinite. Indeed, the author, in the beginnings of composition, may have had the same feeling. Only from hindsight are we prepared to say that the actual second sentence is wholly and inevitably determined, like a point nestled snugly in its curve. Or perhaps what we mean by inevitability is, after all, only a fiction useful to critics. But whether predetermined or simply ad hoc, each additional sentence further conditions the range and relation of those that follow; there is an inverse ratio of decreasing possibilities and increasing constraints. In the exploration of these possibilities, and in the operation of these constraints, is the "coming to be" of story.

Density and Intensity

In the chapter on sentencing, I introduced the notion of density and intensity. These features of the sentence affected the way we could go through it; they interfered with, delayed its course. As we get further into a story, as we experience more and more of its sentences, we cannot help being affected by their predominant thickness or thinness. Normally these features would be described, in more detail, as part of the style. While no one would want to claim that the style is separable from the story, and while many articles have been written to prove that the style *is* the story, I think a slightly different perspective can be gained by forgetting the term *style*—just for now. Instead, I'd ask you to reconceive of syntactic habits and kinds of dictions as forms of interference that we "appreciate" by and through the way we assimilate fiction.

What is it like, for example, to read mostly thin sentences? Note that we are only speaking syntactically and are postponing the question of diction. Nothing prevents a syntactically simple sentence from baffling a reader with hard words. But we might say that the prose of most advertisements and instruction manuals is purposefully thin so as to make both physical and cognitive closure as automatic as possible. Even so, the meaning of, let us say, a cookbook direction may be either instantly perceived, or fumblingly grasped, or altogether missed. What happens depends on a variety of factors, such as the referential precision of the writer and the previous experience of the reader. In imaginative prose, the question is even more complicated. For example, suppose we take a sequence like this:

> He went into the diner. There was an empty stool, so he sat down. He didn't say anything.

With only these sentences to go on, we don't know whether we are reading a second grader or a Hemingway. But so far, we are getting only minimal resistance to the forward movement of the eye and thought. Physical closure is easy, and so, it seems, is cognitive closure. Perhaps the only interference is from a competing voice within our own heads, saying, "What is the point of all this?"

But what happens when we know we are reading a serious artist whose sentences are relatively thin by design? Modification and elaboration may be severely rationed, but this does not mean that the information quotient is low or that the reading is easy. I'll reserve Hemingway—the too obvious example—and ask you to look at a quotation from Raymond Carver. It is from a story about an unemployed salesman, Earl Obert, whose wife "had gone to work nights as a waitress at a twenty-four-hour coffee shop."

> One night, when he was drinking, Earl decided to stop by the coffee shop and have something to eat. He wanted to see where Doreen worked, and he wanted to see if he could order something on the house. . . .
>
> . . . Two men in business suits, their ties undone, their collars open, sat down next to him and asked for coffee. As Doreen walked away with

the coffeepot, one of the men said to the other, "Look at the ass on that. I don't believe it." . . .

. . .

Doreen put the sandwich in front of Earl. Around the sandwich there were French fries, coleslaw, dill pickle.

"Anything else?" she said. "A glass of milk?"

He didn't say anything. He shook his head when she kept standing there.

"I'll get you more coffee," she said.

She came back with the pot and poured coffee for him and for the two men. Then she picked up a dish and turned to get some ice cream. She reached down into the container and with the dipper began to scoop up the ice cream. The white skirt yanked against her hips and crawled up her legs. What showed was girdle, and it was pink, thighs that were rumpled and gray and a little hairy, and veins that spread in a berserk display.

The two men sitting beside Earl exchanged looks. One of them raised his eyebrows. The other man grinned and kept looking at Doreen over his cup as she spooned chocolate syrup over the ice cream. Earl got up, leaving his food, and headed for the door. He heard her call his name, but he kept going.[1]

Clearly these sentences have some density, and clearly their character has a lot to do with their diction. But we can't help noticing the unusual extent to which Carver avoids many opportunities to thicken his sentences. We could imagine greater density being achieved in one or both of two ways: either by combining the given propositions into longer sentences, as in:

1. Coming back with the pot, she poured coffee for him and the two men, and then, picking up a dish, she turned to get some ice cream. As she reached down into the container, scooping up ice cream with the dipper, her white skirt yanked against her hips, crawled up her legs, and showed pink girdle, rumpled thighs—gray and a little hairy —and veins that spread in a berserk display.

or by embedding more propositions into a given sentence, as in:

2. With her neck stiffened by the looks she was getting, she reached down into the pit of the container, and with the scoop extending

1. Carver, "They're Not Your Husband," 20–21.

from her hand like some metal flipper, began to gouge out curled hunks of ice cream.

The point is not the relative goodness or badness of these versions, but simply their feasibility. Also, I will leave to my colleagues the sort of knowledgeable and inspired analysis required to describe the full significance of these stylistic options. My point is that each version argues a different authorial process, a different reading experience, and finally a different story.

Specifically, I would have you note that in both of the variants, the interferences to physical closure are multiplied. Cognitive closure—both immediate and deferred—may not be greatly complicated in the first alternative, though surely it involves a different gestalt of perceptions. In the second alternative, there appear to be more data, more things to note and to hold in relation, but are we really working harder than we do in the original text? As we read Carver's own prose, we become aware of much that's unsaid. For example, what is the husband thinking as he observes the other man's wink? Why is it that he doesn't speak up? We are getting, as we'll get ever more strongly, the impression that this man can't articulate what goes on inside him. Carver wants us to know that Earl's powers of self-examination and self-understanding are so poorly focused they hardly exist. Of course we, as readers, have been primed with carefully selected, highly focused slides of information, all waiting for their cumulative significance to be made clear—to us, if not to Earl. For us, a sentence like "He didn't say anything" has already gained unstated meaning, and will itself become part of the unstated meaning of sentences to come. Borrowing a phrase from the dramatists, we might say that this sequence has a complicated "subtext": the wife's dutiful acceptance of the menial task that supports her unemployed husband, the two men's casual vulgarity, the husband's vague, misguided, but driving sense of shame. And that is only the first level of implication. Beyond that, we sense, even on a first reading, something chilling in the husband's pretense of being "just a customer." These thin sentences offer a kind of anomaly—easy physical closure, fairly easy immediate cognitive closure, but far from easy, even deliberately difficult, deferred cognitive closure. I suppose the classic case of this anomaly is Hemingway's "Hills Like White Elephants."

But what is it like to read an author who *has* availed himself of opportunities to thicken his prose? James and Faulkner come to mind. The
texture of their language seems almost palpable to the mind's touch. To
say it another way, their rich style is an obtrusive one. While it might
seem that we could be bored by Carver's lean style (as we surely are by
imitations of Hemingway), we are in fact kept alert by having to look
through the interstices for the meaning—and by being rewarded for
doing so. But with writers like Faulkner and James—well, the holes are
stopped up with *more* language. Of course I do not mean that Faulkner
restricts his reader's imagination more than Carver does. The power to
stir the imagination is not a function of density or of any other single
feature of the sentence; it is a function of the author's own imaginative
power, which may find its best expression in either a thin style or a
dense one. I would use these terms only descriptively. I would say, for
example, that Carver teases us into collaboration by noting the salient
points of a scene we must work to fill in, while Faulkner makes us work
hard to take in all the points he's hidden in a field of more points. When
Carver's imagination flags—or should I say overexpands?—the scenes
dissolve into quirks of phrase. The ebb and flow of imaginative power
in any writer might be described in terms of how the thinness or the
density works at different times, and of course there are many studies
which coordinate the way an author's language looks to us and the way
reality looks to that author. Faulkner and James would be excellent examples to use now, but I think it would be better again to choose a contemporary writer about whom we haven't so many stored-up impres-
sions. Someone like Jerry Bumpus:

> You believe the golf ball achieves maximum velocity at impact, but in
> fact this occurs several yards from the tee, and at the moment of greatest
> speed, when at its finest as a golf ball, it is flat, squashed against the air, an
> odd oblong resembling in my excellent photographs a forward-leaning
> ghost stumbling through space.[2]

Bumpus' stories depend on ingenuity of invention. His more densely
textured sentences, with their dependent clauses and serial modifiers,
put in all the details of the map—and it's a Salvador Dali terrain. It
would be superfluous for us to add even the smallest detail. We have the

2. Bumpus, "Our Golf Balls," 14.

feeling that our retinas have been painted over; we can't see more than we're given. The words exhaust expression—or at least all the expression the content can bear, or the writer attain. This isn't to say that there's not more to the story than the print on the page. Interpretations are never foreclosed. But it *is* to say that our first experience is not one of filling in, but of adjusting to what's amply provided. The hindrances to physical closure are the crowded phrases, which are of course one of the delights of these sentences. The hindrances to cognitive closure are the difficulties of remaining imaginatively equal to the demands of an eccentric vision. Obviously, deferred closure will be easier for some readers than for others. It helps if you have a mind like Jerry Bumpus', or if you have read many other contemporary writers who picture the world in a similar way.

Perhaps you will recall now, from the earlier chapter on sentences, what happens when we momentarily—and arbitrarily—separate diction from syntax. There are of course analyses of style which point out ratios of concrete to abstract words, Saxon to Roman roots, demotic to formal diction, etc. And we know that readers will have different kinds of reading experiences with, say, colloquial prose, alien jargon, newspaperese, or dialect transcription. But these are gross distinctions. They may be less important to us than ones that are harder to make—and chancier.

I asked you earlier to consider a shady but possible distinction between functional words like *said* and affectively more loaded words like *moaned*. We're presuming largely upon norms of reading experience, cultural conditioning, and language usage. There are also important differences between the conventions of speech and those of a particular literary period or genre. But let us temporarily assume that we can talk about the kind and degree of affective stimulus a word conveys—or can be made to convey. Questions leap up: are we responding to 1) an emotion trigger built into the word itself by our experience with it in the past, or 2) a referent to which the word merely points and which, in real life, would have moved us? William Gass would argue that the second is certainly not true—at least not in fine literature—and that the first is true only if we allow the artist the widest discretion and power to recondition a word through the arrangement of context. For our purposes, it will do if we can agree that some words—either of themselves, or as loaded or unloaded by the artist's design—carry more affective freight than others. We must, of course, realize that the emotional power of any given sentence or even phrase is hardly to be explained as the summed affect of the individual words, and we must also admit that an apparently neutral sentence, like "He didn't say anything" *could* have more affective freight than "He murdered his wife." Yet wouldn't we be inclined to say that the words of the first sentence must acquire their power through a stratagem of the author, while his art must be even more active to neutralize "murder"?

In addition to such affective stimuli, we considered the possibility of words carrying special ability to pique our curiosity, to arouse the intellect. These may be simply words we're surprised to see, or words we associate with acts of inference, comparison, etc. (such as "thus," "for this reason," "because"). But of course sentences in fiction give us a complex experience of both affective *and* perceptual activity. Going back to Jerry Bumpus' sentence about the golf ball, who could or would want to separate the "*how*'s that?" (of maximum velocity at impact, "odd oblong," and photographs of a ghost) from the "like *that!*" (of "squashed against the air" and "stumbling through space"). Indeed, the phrase that gives me the greatest delight—"at its finest as a golf ball"—generates a number of agreeable affects, some of which surely come from perception. The word "finest" is loaded with pleasing connotations, carrying with it an aura of excellence and approval; applied to a golf ball, it generates a quirk of amusement—also pleasing; the phrase "at its finest" may echo self-realization lingo, perhaps even a Churchillian rhetoric ("their finest hour"), but its general quality is burlesque—an inflated language applied to a trivial object. Perhaps these, and undoubtedly other, recognitions occur, making for personification. The golf ball is a human hero—and the story takes off.

Going back to Carver, we might fasten on the word "rumpled" in "thighs that were rumpled and gray." It conveys a fact to us; we now know something we didn't know before. But, to borrow again from the linguists, "rumpled" has a plus-inanimate, minus-human signification, and customarily goes with "girdle" rather than with "thighs." The dislocation is easily adjusted to, but not before it has heightened the pejorative affect of "rumpled" here, and not before it has honed our recognition of what dowdy flesh can look like—or, perhaps more specifically, how it looks to Earl now. Impossible, then, to separate the affective and the intellectual stimuli we receive from a word, much less from a group of words. Poe—speaking of "beauty" and "terror" on the one hand, and "ratiocination" on the other—may have been the last to try.

Having reviewed both density and intensity, we might speculate a little in a cautious way. Could it be that in a dense-textured prose, the intensities are likely to be the immediate effect of the words on the page? In a thin-textured prose, it may be that the diction yields many high-intensity words, but it may also be that we are moved or stimulated in ways and at times that aren't so obvious. In stories like Carver's and Hemingway's, density is normally low and intensity is kept down through the deliberate avoidance of both emotionally charged and intellectually difficult words. A very great deal goes on off the page—but is still dependent upon what is on it. The unsaid is called forth by the said. There are times, in both "They're Not Your Husband" and "Hills Like White Elephants," when the low intensity of the words that are said makes us all the more aware of the high intensity of the words that are not said. Of course the artist has no control over the words he didn't write. Indeed, they may never be fully articulated by the reader, and certainly not on a first reading. Therefore, the intensities will be less precisely controlled, less verbally triggered, and more dependent on the reader's own sensibility and experience of life than those triggered by the abundantly said. Before we can "read" the unsaid in "Hills Like White Elephants," don't we have to know, from some other source, that there's such a thing as abortion? That is the high-intensity word which is deliberately kept off the page.

Density as a function of syntax, and intensity as a function of diction together comprise a world—first spied in the sentence—which is infinitely varied in the relationships—obvious or hidden—which may exist among its elements. Together they create the texture of the prose, and together they interfere with closure.

Texture

I left you wondering whether "Rip Van Winkle" wasn't really a story about some mountains. In the beginning of that story, we were taken on a voyage up the Hudson and back to a time "of great antiquity." When we at last meet Rip, he is nestled in the heart of old New York State. In the heart, too, of enwrapping prose. Below is a paragraph which we encounter well along into story:

[1] In a long ramble of the kind on a fine autumnal day, Rip had unconsciously scrambled to one of the highest parts of the Kaatskill mountains. [2] He was after his favourite sport of squirrel shooting and the still solitudes had echoed and re-echoed with the reports of his gun. [3] Panting and fatigued he threw himself, late in the afternoon, on a green knoll, covered with mountain herbage, that crowned the brow of a precipice. [4] From an opening between the trees he could overlook all the lower country for many a mile of rich woodland. [5] He saw at a distance the lordly Hudson, far, far below him, moving on its silent but majestic course, with the reflection of a purple cloud, or the sail of a lagging bark here and there sleeping on its glassy bosom, and at last losing itself in the blue highlands.[3]

None of these sentences really holds us up, yet none gives us closure too quickly. The long ramble is part of a series of three prepositional phrases, and the scramble takes us over three more. There's no hurry in the next sentence either, but time for an echo of "echoed and re-echoed." Then "he threw himself, late in the afternoon." There hangs Rip, thrown, almost suspended in air, as the late afternoon passes, before he lands "on a green knoll." He's so high in the mountains that now he, like them, overlooks the country below, "for many a mile." We're into a story that's going to add a "mile of rich woodland," at no extra cost. Here now is the last sentence, rearranged to emphasize its density:

He saw   the lordly Hudson
    at a distance
    far, far below him
        moving
                on its silent but majestic course
              with the reflection of a purple cloud
        or⟶the sail of a lagging bark
                      here and there
                sleeping
          ..[and]··⟍   on its glassy bosom
  and⟶losing itself
       at last
       in the blue highlands.

3. Irving, "Rip Van Winkle," 32–33.

There is a good deal of embedding here. (Interestingly enough, there is also an instance of the overdetermined, "false" parallelism we noted in the Gordimer sentence.) Grammatical layering serves the effect of visual layering: this sentence guides our perception as the eye is guided deeper into a scene. The ruling aesthetic here is that of the romantic landscape painting, where the flatness of the canvas is transcended by the illusion of perspective. Our eye follows the winding path that leads into the "distance." While not denying the relevance of the pictorial mode— likely very conscious on Irving's part[4]—I'd like to stress the ontology of fiction. What we are assimilating is secondarily a picture or a vista; primarily we are having an experience of syntax. In this case, it's fairly dense, holding off closure, slowing the rate at which we apprehend wholeness. It's a story that fills us with a sense of place—all those prepositional phrases!—long views and long times.

But what about intensity? The paragraph contains 144 words. Of these, at least 6 seem to me to carry some affective weight: "fine," "favorite," "painting," "fatigued," "lordly," "majestic." Within the conventions of picturesque prose, the following phrases acquire positive, "romantic" affects: "long ramble," "autumnal day," "still solitudes," "green knoll," "mountain herbage," "rich woodland," "lagging bark," and "glassy bosom." Because of their association with a context of sovereignty (earlier attached to the mountains), certain other words rise in prominence: "crowned," "lordly," "majestic," and "purple." But if we think Irving deals only in placid affects, we should note that the very next paragraph, describing the "deep mountain glen," reveals negative (or perhaps I should say conventionally sinister) affect: "wild," "lonely," "shagged," "fragments," "impending," "dark," "heavy," and "terrors." Irving is working comfortably within the traditions of the romantic sublime. But that is a tradition relying heavily on a conventionalized set of affects, evoked by a set of tag words. If we savor the tradition, our experience of "getting through" is enriched. If not, the experience may seem rather tedious—at least insofar as it has been conditioned by verbal intensity.

Now let me get you out of the mountains and onto the sea. Here we are in the midst of Crane's story:

4. See James T. Callow, *Kindred Spirits: Knickerbocker Writers and American Artists, 1807–1855* (Chapel Hill, 1967).

[1] The voyagers scanned the shore. [2] A conference was held in the boat. [3] "Well," said the captain, "if no help is coming, we might better try a run through the surf right away. [4] If we stay out here much longer, we will be too weak to do anything for ourselves at all." [5] The others silently acquiesced in this reasoning. [6] The boat was headed for the beach. [7] The correspondent wondered if none ever ascended the tall wind-tower, and if then they never looked seaward. [8] This tower was a giant, standing with its back to the plight of the ants. [9] It represented in a degree, to the correspondent, the serenity of nature amid the struggles of the individual—nature in the wind, and nature in the vision of men. [10] She did not seem cruel to him then, nor beneficent, nor treacherous, nor wise. [11] But she was indifferent, flatly indifferent. [12] It is, perhaps, plausible that a man in this situation, impressed with the unconcern of the universe, should see the innumerable flaws of his life and have them taste wickedly in his mind and wish for another chance. [13] A distinction between right and wrong seems absurdly clear to him, then, in this new ignorance of the grave-edge, and he understands that if he were given another opportunity he would mend his conduct and his words, and be better and brighter during an introduction, or at a tea.[5]

Clearly there are times when Crane wants very swift closure, as in the sentences numbered 1, 2, 5, 6, and 11. Frequent commas seem to emphasize the simpler units within the longer sentences, but #13 still takes some "going through." It is prosy and full of compoundings. It closes a paragraph full of high-intensity (and mostly negatively charged) words like "weak," "giant," "plight," "serenity," "struggles," "cruel," "beneficent," "treacherous," "wise," "indifferent," "flaws," "wickedly," "absurdly," "grave-edge." How, then, are we struck, at the end of a gradually thickening density, a relatively high intensity, to come upon those surprisingly neutral words "introduction" and "tea." The deflation, which is abrupt and ironic, serves an unmerciful truth. Serves, I should say, this story.

Finally, in the Mexico of "Flowering Judas," we find the role of density and intensity so important that it can hardly be discussed apart from another aspect of story. For, as we attempt to explain the way we internalize the effects of density and intensity, we need to remember that we are also getting incremental information. The story reveals itself piecemeal to the reader, and yet exists permanently throughout the text as a whole. In the simplest sense, linearity of discourse is a function of the

5. Crane, "The Open Boat," 88.

way we apprehend density and intensity: one word, or phrase, at a time, in a left-to-right orientation. But of course the story correlate, the meaning which exists in the mind rather than on the page, may be regarded either as a series of events, a sequence of ideas, a movement from and to, or it may be regarded as an overall design initially perceived quirk by quirk, but finally perceived and retained as an integrated figure, a holistic shape. In my chapter on the history of story criticism, I discussed in some detail the difference between a theory of the story based on the notion of linearity (the development of a plot, the preparation for the epiphany, the conditioning of an attitude) and one based on the notion of spatiality (the pattern of interlocking images, the features of symmetry and contrast, the all-suffusing mood). All stories have both a linear and a spatial dimension, but one or the other may seem to predominate in a given story.

Linearity

Plot as trajectory is perhaps a primitive notion—or rather a notion appropriate to so-called primitive fiction. An agent who commands our interest is hurled through a series of adventures to land in either significant defeat or fulfilling success. That trajectory may be described as a series of episodes, like a stone skipped on water; it may be seen as a deadset pursuit, rather like a beeline; or it may be perceived as a subtle relationship of curves, a sort of braid. Different stories will suggest different analogies.

Here, for example, is D. S. Mirsky characterizing Chekhov's stories in the language of curves: these fictions, he says, describe an arc of "emotional process," at first indistinguishable from a straight line; but then "an infinitesimal touch . . . gives a hint at the direction the story is going to take. It is then repeated as a leit-motif, and at each repetition the true equation of the curve becomes more important, and it ends by shooting away in a direction very different from that of the original straight line."[6] For her own special purposes with regard to the lyrical short story, Eileen Baldeshwiler builds on Mirsky to say that "the plot line will hereafter consist . . . of tracing complex emotions to a closing cadence utterly unlike the reasoned resolution of the conventional cause-and-effect narrative."[7]

6. D. S. Mirsky, quoted in Baldeshwiler, "The Lyric Short Story," 204.
7. Baldeshwiler, *ibid.*, 206.

One thinks of the detective story and the heroic romance as end-directed fictions, but even so subtle a writer as Eudora Welty uses the notion of the lure along the path. For her, "On some level all stories are stories of search."[8] Of plot, she says, "When it is identifiable in every motion and progression of its own with the motion and progress of simple revelation, then it is at its highest use" (p. 170). Even more interesting here is her emphasis on the linearity of the process which brings the story into being. Having, as she does, a commitment to the organic view of art—that it "grows" or "evolves"—she believes the process to be as uni-directional as the transformation of the bud into the flower. "I hear the arrow of time exists," she says, "and I feel quite certain, by every instinct, so does the arrow of creation. . . . A story is not the same thing when it ends that it was when it began. Something happens—the writing of it. It *becomes*. And as a story becomes, I believe we as readers understand by becoming too—by enjoying" (p. 162). Thus, for her, "plot" is a multivalent term. It is first of all the "arrow of creation," the genetic program of the author's act of creation. It is also the universal "search" that each story particularizes. Finally, plot is the arrow of appreciation, the change that "happens to" the reader in the act of reading. It is Welty's tendency to shift back and forth between the points of view of writer and reader that both energizes and confuses her theory. But she does give us a broader sense of what "linear" may mean, as a description of both a story's form and a reader's experience.

For a more philosophically careful—and cagey—point of view, we turn back to Ingarden. While stressing that "temporal extension is not an attribute of the literary work itself,"[9] he does feel that once we conceive of parts to any written discourse, we must agree that its value is enhanced if there is an inviolable order of those parts in relation to each other. While not conceived of as "earlier" or "later" in a temporal sense, the relative positions do reflect a principle of sequence. That principle is the "*one-sidedness of conditioning*." Ingarden elaborates:

> Every phase of the literary work (except for the first) shows moments within it which have their foundation outside themselves in moments of a different, "earlier" phase. At the same time, every phase contains within it a system of elements that requires *no* foundation in elements of a different phase. Finally, it contains moments that constitute the basis or foundation

8. Welty, "The Reading and Writing of Short Stories," 170.
9. Ingarden, *The Literary Work of Art*, 305.

of determinate moments of a different, "subsequent" phase. . . . It is precisely through these properties of foundation that the order of "sequence" of phases in a literary work is established. (pp. 310–11)

Now this one-sidedness of conditioning may be illustrated on many levels. Clearly it exists as a grammatical imperative. We have already noted the obvious "sequence signals" which are a sort of economy measure. They allow us to avoid repetition of previously asserted information. The pronoun "he" refers to a previously named male individual. If the story hasn't provided us with that name, then the "he" simply refers back to an "X" that will be, we trust, eventually identified. The direction of reference is as inviolate as the direction of the earth's spin. And then, if the constraint of verisimilitude is working at all (can it ever be totally disregarded?), then there are other "arrows" of experience. The sun rises before it sets. People marry before they divorce. But they don't always think before they speak.

In life, the degree of "necessariness" of sequences is variously determined. In fiction, it is determined by the author acting under certain constraints, which he more or less consciously chooses. Perhaps it is easiest to understand linearity by positing the particular constraint of consistency within the larger constraint of verisimilitude. We're not surprised that a person named Ruth last week is still named Ruth today. And we expect a character named Ruth on page one to be named Ruth on page ten. But if there is some way for the author to make us accept the fact that, on page eleven of his story, the Rowena of page ten becomes the Ligeia of page one, then the author has chosen a set of constraints which challenge verisimilitude. Perhaps we will always wonder whether Poe has chosen to assume his narrator's madness, or whether he intends the dead Ligeia to take over her successor's body. Far more usually, we simply have $Ruth_1$ and $Ruth_2$—the same woman in the ordinary, everyday sense, but a different woman because of what she has seen, felt, experienced in the meantime. All we have is the de facto sequence X_1, X_2, X_3, X_n. Plot is the illusion that this sequence is a necessary arrow of existence. The anticlosure forces—like the felt absence of some part of the grammar of expectation—are those uncertainties and questions which keep us from feeling the end can arrive. Thus the management of anticlosure is guided by the story's peculiar strategy of revelation. As Welty says, successful revelation is plot.

The linearity of "Rip Van Winkle" is suggested by the opening movement from our present point in place and time to the inner reaches of the Hudson and the early days of the province. Once we meet Rip we linger with him in the village, but clearly by way of prelude to a special adventure. Soon we are on the move again, on foot this time, up the mountain, up the gully, through a cleft, and into a hollow. Obviously the order matters. It is an order of ascent. Critics have also pointed out that this series of climbs imitates the arduous entry into a womb—not of termagent wife but of nature and folklore and time.[10] What is fertilized there is imagination. But we will not know that until later.

Though Rip seems to be retracing his steps, going back to the point of beginning, the whole wonder of the story is that he is *not* the same, that nothing is the same except the river and hillside. Thus the trajectory of the story passes, quite literally, through the high point of Rip's encounter/vision/dream and descends through stages of bewilderment. Seeking his home, he finds a strange world. The wonder is that the town he finds is stranger than the mountain he left. What lured him originally was his need to escape the world or "real" responsibility, his affable, genial, willing acquiescence in the marvelous. What lures him back to the town is his need for the familiar supports of identity. Now this is a story in which the constraint of verisimilitude is met—up to a point. Up to the appearance of the strange little man. Thereafter, another constraint helps to condition the prose. We might call it at first the constraint of the source—that German legend of Peter Klaus. Or we might—more appropriately, I think—call it the constraint of theme. That theme takes precedence over other constraints.

I said earlier that $Ruth_1$ of page one is $Ruth_n$ of page ten. Quite clearly the Rip_1 who goes into the mountain is not the Rip_n who comes down. Even *he* knows it.

> "God knows," exclaimed he, at his wit's end, "I'm not myself—I'm somebody else—. . . . I was myself last night; but I fell asleep on the mountain and they've changed my gun and every thing's changed—and I'm changed—and I can't tell what's my name, or who I am!"[11]

Finally, the identity of Rip_1 and Rip_n is very tenuously asserted by the

---

10. See Philip Young, "Fallen from Time: Rip Van Winkle," in *Three Bags Full* (New York, 1973).

11. Irving, "Rip Van Winkle," 38–39.

claims of genealogy and (very importantly) by the story constraint of consistency. But the changes matter. Rip_1 was a young adult in the prime of life, made vastly uncomfortable by his unfitness to perform as father, husband, and farmer. Rip_n is an old man, past the age of responsibility, tolerantly allowed *now* to perform the function for which he has always been fit. For which he has been prepared and to which he has been initiated by his dip into myth. Now that others see him as useless for real work, he can become—a teller of tales. Which happens to be, by the way, just what Irving is.

If it is true that we need to meet Rip_1 before we can meet and appreciate the significance of Rip_n, then we've established a "here-to-there." We've experienced a one-directional sequence of information. An arrow of story. An arrow of understanding and enjoyment.

In "The Open Boat," Crane gives the utmost urgency to the act of getting from the leaden waves to the gritty shore. There is the physical, navigational path, and there's also the path of spiritual growth. The primary "who" of this story becomes the correspondent as we begin to see where he's been (unenlightened cynicism), what he's passing through (doubt, despair, and resentment), and where he's going to get (resignation and fellow feeling). For the characters, getting to the land means saving their lives. It also comes to mean surviving with knowledge. What does it mean for us?

The paragraph quoted earlier takes us through one phase of the correspondent's growth in understanding. He moves from a view of the waves as "wrongfully and barbarously abrupt and tall" ($attitude_n$) to a view of them as coldly indifferent ($attitude_n$). The story offers many perceptual sequences undergone by the characters themselves—some of them short and repetitive, such as the frequent experiencing of visual error and faulty inference gradually corrected toward a truer perception. They continually misread—then correct—what they see. There's a one-sided conditioning, a necessary order to this sequence; it gives us a feeling of linearity. Overall, of course, the grammar of expectation offers a crucial choice (they will or will not get to shore) that must be resolved before we'll accept closure. The fact that we will keep reading to "find out what happens" is, of course, the simplest and most powerful function of linearity.

Spatiality

Basic as it is, linearity has its limits. A line may be made by a moving dot, but if you plot a series of points, you make a design in space. The points may appear seriatim, but the design will appear as a whole. And once we switch to the language of graphics, we are on our way to a whole new set of metaphors. It is appropriate now to consider an approach to the story that deemphasizes its linearity in order to stress its shape.

In "Spatial Form in Modern Literature," a controversial article when it was written in the forties, Joseph Frank tells what happens to art—and aesthetics—when the diachronic feature of sequential plot is subordinated to the synchronic feature of spatial design. Even though he deals only with certain modern poems and novels, his argument has influenced, directly or indirectly, many critics of the short story. In part, he says that:

> Esthetic form in modern poetry . . . is based on a space-logic that demands a complete re-orientation in the reader's attitude towards language. Since the primary reference of any word-group is to something inside the poem itself, language in modern poetry is really reflexive: the meaning-relationship is completed only by the simultaneous perception in space of word-groups which, when read consecutively in time, have no comprehensible relation to each other. . . . Modern poetry asks its readers to suspend the process of individual reference temporarily until the entire pattern of internal references can be apprehended as a unity.[12]

The case would be overstated if applied to most (though not some contemporary) short stories; normally the consecutive order of words does make sense, but it may contain signals which are related to each other in a way distinct from the syntactic flow of the prose. Within the story, they may constitute an internal organization of parts related to each other in a static design like the pattern on a carpet. This design is held firm in the overseeing mind as the eye crosses a carpet of pages, an inch at a time. In the realm of short story criticism alone, how many countless studies of "patterns of imagery" and "recurrent motifs" owe their theoretical inspiration to Frank!

12. Frank, "Spatial Form in Modern Literature," 229–30.

As I stated earlier, all stories have a dimension of spatiality. Rip Van Winkle's experience may follow the path of his steps, but our appreciation of the story not only follows his track, but spreads gradually to include the design of his path. The shape of "The Open Boat" may be that of embedded circles of awareness, from (though not necessarily beginning with) the narrowest and most human-centered cry to (and in this case probably ending with) the broadest, nearest equivalent to "the great sea's voice."

This perception of the whole, which is something like the perception of the figure latent in the numbered dots, is made easier or harder by many features of a story. But the ease or difficulty of discerning the figure is also a function of the reader's experience with fiction in general, and in particular with fiction that emphasizes spatiality. Highly spatialized stories are more common in contemporary fiction than, for example, in nineteenth-century fiction. Faced with one, a beginning student will often try to reconstruct one or more linear progressions (with or without the help of the author). More sophisticated critics will sometimes look for ways to apply Frank's spatiality to the linguistic "stuff" of the story.

I've been saving a discussion of "Flowering Judas" because it begs for—and indeed has already received—just this kind of study. Beverly Gross's article "The Poetic Narrative: A Reading of 'Flowering Judas'" identifies a repeated figure of syntactic arrangement in Porter's story.[13] Over and over again, says Gross, Porter uses coordinating conjunctions to link a simple statement of Laura's situation or perceptions with a counter-statement giving the author's often ironic elaboration or concealed appraisal of what has just been stated. For example,

> [Braggioni's parents] gave him the love and knowledge of music, thus: and under the rip of his thumbnail, the strings of the instrument complain like exposed nerves.[14]

Here, according to Gross, the pattern allows a counterpointing of illusion and disillusion. She finds this linguistic/thematic entity turning up again and again, and therefore she admits that it is first perceived tem-

13. Gross, "The Poetic Narrative," 129–39.
14. Porter, "Flowering Judas," 98.

porally. But her stress is on its re-occurrence, on the essential oneness of all its separate appearances, and therefore on its static presentness throughout.

From my point of view, what Gross is noticing is a special characteristic of the density (*i.e.*, a typical use of subordinating clauses) and intensity (*i.e.*, a typical use of harshly true adjectives—loaded with negative affect). The constancy of these features conditions our reading experience sentence by sentence, but it also, eventually, leads to our perceiving a design. Here is one portion of it:

> [1] She is not at home in the world. [2] Every day she teaches children who remain strangers to her, though she loves their tender round hands and their charming opportunist savagery. [3] She knocks at unfamiliar doors not knowing whether a friend or a stranger shall answer, and even if a known face emerges from the sour gloom of that unknown interior, still it is the face of a stranger. [4] No matter what this stranger says to her, nor what her message to him, the very cells of her flesh reject knowledge and kinship in one monotonous word. [5] No. [6] No. [7] No. [8] She draws her strength from this one holy talismanic word which does not suffer her to be led into evil. [9] Denying everything, she may walk anywhere in safety, she looks at everything without amazement. (p. 97)

So far in the story, we have been present in the house of this woman who "is not at home in the world." In the direct action of the story, she will allow Braggioni to sing, will clean and oil his gun, send him back to his revolution and his wife, and then go to bed—and dream—and wake in fright. We learn about Laura's daily life and her few, abortive, denied romances through a curious maneuver. The active present tense blends into the historical present, so that this particular evening fuses with many like it. Flashbacks to specific prior events are signaled by a shift to the past tense, but soon we are back in the present that holds the past like an insect in amber. By the time we reach the passage I've quoted, it is clear that the present can be used in two ways. "Laura feels a slow chill, a purely physical sense of danger. . . ." And "No dancer dances more beautifully than Laura walks. . . ." The present is inhabited by Laura, whose thoughts we sometimes share. But it is also inhabited—with her uncaring permission—by Braggioni, by "the author," and, in spirit, by Eugenio. All are critics of Laura. The men ask for her love, for

her compassion, maybe only for her recognition of them as fellow beings. "The author," tight-lipped, restrained, patiently reveals Laura's
fear of life, her substitution of mechanical principle for human response.

The statement "she is not at home in the world" does not describe
one event which follows another, but a condition which is constant
throughout the story. What changes or develops is our understanding
of what the statement implies about the quality of Laura's "being in the
world." We learned in the second sentence of the story that Laura has
"her own house," a place which can be invaded by unwelcome visitors.
Now we are told that she is not at home anywhere in the world, that all
people, regardless of whether they feel hate, love, or indifference toward
her, are seen as tolerated intruders; they are neutralized, equated, denied by her will. She can "love" ideals, lace, the round hands of children; she is afraid to love men, women, and the children themselves.
The oxymoron "charming . . . savagery," the play, in the third sentence,
on "not knowing," "known," and "unknown"; the "no," "nor," and "re-
ject" of the fourth; the three staccato "No's" that follow—together yield
a high incidence of high-intensity words, all charged with her negation
of life. The eighth sentence, with its echo of the Lord's Prayer, replaces
"Our Father" with a "word." And the word is not *Love* but *No*. We'll
have to consider the religious implications when we look at the closure
of the story, but it is already clear that Laura has committed a blasphemy. The world itself is reduced to that "everything" which she can
deny, that "anywhere" she can be without being at home.

Our progress through this story is certainly, in many ways, a linear
progression. If we arrange the young captain, the brown shock-haired
youth, and Eugenio as potential lovers 1, 2, and 3, we may be surprised
to see that they are introduced in reverse order of sexual demand. We
must understand why this sequence is necessary. But predominantly, I
think, we have an experience of selective and keen intensities of diction
and qualifications of syntax. With each sentence we see another detail in
the design of life denial, another petal of the flowering Judas. By the
end—but this is a matter for the chapter on closure.

CHAPTER FIVE

Getting Out of Story

• • •

Reading is an activity disparate from others; it introduces us to an integrated system of postulates that "make" a world ontologically discontinuous with that world which isn't verbally mediated, as well as from those worlds that are mediated by other discourses; and it acts upon us in ways that may parallel but are always phenomenologically different from the way our own world makes us respond. So importunate is story, that it not only displaces and competes with other periods of highly determined living, but indeed puts us through one such phase. That phase may be described as a reality warp within the reader's life; it may be thought of as the assimilation of the reality warp which is the story itself, or it may be explained by spelling out—as I have in the previous chapters—the way we respond to the effects of density, intensity, linearity, and spatiality. These mental activities of reading include direct appreciation of the physical body of the language, intermittent correlations with personal memory, prefigurings and anticipations evoked by the grammar of expectation in general and by particular modelings of thought and feeling, evolving judgments, triggered emotions, tangential daydreams—but the list goes on in the direction of one's own theory of what fiction is or does. Whatever the theory, I would contend that it describes, for the short story, a rhythm of closure. And I would add that the commanding difference between this form and others is, as is all too obvious, its length—but its length as the unique prerequisite and determinant of a rhythm definite enough to delay or even to displace life's other tides—till it's had its swell—till the author says "stop."

Typologies

Previous attempts to explain the wholeness of story have relied on typologies drawn from various areas of human experience. Remarkably—and very significantly—these areas represent a common rather than an abstruse knowledge; we speak of stories in terms of elementary school graphs, popular superstition, and ordinary sentences. The one exception may be the model based on genre, which is the literary critic's substitute for science. My own description of the way stories work will be based on the very simplest model of all, organic periodicity. But by way of introduction, I'll review some of the other typologies that critics have used.

Geometry

Already we've noticed how the diction of geometry—of lines, points, and convergences—has been used to describe the forms of fiction. Plots rise, turn, or criss-cross. John Barth, in his story "Lost in the Funhouse," has made a plaything of the traditional plot formula, which he pauses to graph on the page:

This diagram fits the traditional concept of conflict-and-resolution, "rising" and "falling" action, and final "denouement." Stories "end" when this pattern is completed.[2]

We would need another sort of diagram to fit the modern notion of "epiphany," even of "open-endedness." For in the crudest, most generalized terms, it is usual to regard the traditional story, descending from Poe, as "plotted" and "closed," and the modern story, descending from Joyce, as "unplotted" and "open." Whether one speaks of the shift from overt to indirect method, from objective to subjective frames of reference, from character-in-action to creation-of-atmosphere, from formulaic to anti-formal aesthetics—the result is that the second-named category is harder to graph.

---

1. Barth, "Lost in the Funhouse," 95.
2. For a review of several such graphic models, including Freitag's, see Dollerup, "Concepts of 'Tension,' 'Intensity,' and 'Suspense' in Short-Story Theory."

Not that it can't be. A. L. Bader spends an article trying to prove that "the reader must supply the missing parts of the traditional plot in many modern stories,"[3] and Theodore A. Stroud contends that "in most of the stories today, as in previous centuries, the completeness results from the units or episodes in a story being combined to make credible a 'change' in one of the characters."[4] Both men are committed to a conservative view of the formal properties of the story. They see these properties as definitive of the genre and therefore necessarily there, whether in plain sight or in hiding. And I believe these critics and others like them are right about the genetic stability of the short story as a species of fiction. But their models are drawn with a straight-edge. Their periods fall within ruled squares, so neatly plotted, so essentially schematic, that they can never be more useful (though perhaps never less valid) than a Euclidean law, a Newtonian force. Closure is the meeting of the apple with the ground.

Behavioral Sciences

It takes a later and a bigger law to tell us how straight lines bend in nature; and it has long been obvious that they do so in psychology and culture. I'd like now to consider some views of open and closed form that derive from a "newer" science. In 1958, Robert M. Adams published a collection of essays entitled *Strains of Discord: Studies in Literary Openness.* In one of these essays, "Romantic Openness and the Unconscious," he suggests a connection between a historical, national attitude toward life, and the literature produced within that cultural climate: "[Since Whitman] American writing has included a strain of enthusiastic, receptive, indeterminate openness to experience which finds expression in loose, unstructured form."[5] He goes on to specify that "the open form is literary form . . . which includes a major unresolved conflict with the intent of displaying its unresolvedness" (p. 13). Such "unresolvedness" is, he contends, a matter of deciding *against* resolution. His "un-" is indicative. "Openness" becomes a deliberate refusal to comply with expected forms of closure; it is a refusal conceived of positively, as an avoidance for the sake of a gain. Adams even lists the more common

3. Bader, "The Structure of the Modern Short Story," 110.
4. Stroud, "A Critical Approach to the Short Story," 119.
5. Adams, *Strains of Discord*, 183.

reasons for deciding to "unresolve": "to explore a philosophy"; "to gain a perspective"; "to fulfill the requirements of a style" (p. 206). "Explore," "gain," "fulfill"—his verbs manifest a destiny within the territories of organized meaning—thought, vision, and style. That destiny is one of civilizing, of "summariz[ing] and clarify[ing] the common experience of the race." Some fiction gives us the results of this imperative; *i.e.*, some fiction settles the land. Other fiction scouts ahead, to "report on the unfamiliar" (p. 210). There is much to be said for this approach to story, but it is not so innovative as it seems. Adams, after all, conceives of "openness" in a very "closed" way—that is, he defines, illustrates, and justifies it in relation to the old linear model: conflict, leading to complication, ending in resolution.

Alan Friedman, sensing this limitation in Adams, has looked for a more genuine model of openness. He finds it in the fluidity of experience. Novels, he says, show a "stream of events," taking the form of "assaults [on] and offers [to]" the initially innocent character, who responds in feeling and/or in action. There is a "stream of conscience."[6] Gradually, the character becomes more experienced, but continually, endlessly, he or she is open to, or exposed to, yet another assault or offer from life. Friedman wants to locate his model for fiction in the "real" world, but realizes that the best he can do is locate it in what he believes are "real" attitudes toward the world. These attitudes, he says, have changed. We now see the world as an open-ended imposition on man, rather than as a battle he may win or lose. Novels that are true to this perception show their characters under the necessity of responding (or learning how to respond) to whatever the author-created world throws them. This response is an "ethical" one, because it may be judged either appropriate (right) or inappropriate (wrong) according to one's system for rendering man and circumstances accountable. Thus, the view that experience is a never-ending assault on innocence, requiring always a never-final response, leads to a model of open-endedness within the domain of ethics or behavioral science. That assumption in turn leads to a model of narrative structure. As our novelists think of us, we never strike a truce with life; it always spurns or invites us anew. "Endings," then, are purely discretionary; they can occur whenever the author

6. Friedman, Alan, *The Turn of the Novel*, xiii–xviii, 9–14.

thinks he has made his point about the kinds of "assaults and offers" the world is likely to provide, and the kinds of responses his character is likely to make. As Friedman sees it, the problem of the modern author, including the modern short-story author, is how to "end without closing." [7]

Now, just as Adams' conservatism may also be seen in such short story critics as Bader and Stroud, so, too, Friedman's "modernism" re-echoes in H. E. Bates and Nadine Gordimer, who argue that the story has been influenced by the "new" clichés: modern malaise, occasioned by a loss of faith in orderly and contained systems of thought, leading to a view of life and art as fragmented and inconclusive. Thus closure is the maturation point of a growing conviction—about what it means for character X to be alive in world Y. Later I will return to these views of openness in order to question their interchangeable application to stories and novels. But first I'd like to review another group of important typologies, those based on models of time, genre, and language.

Millennia

Temporal finality is Frank Kermode's subject in *The Sense of an Ending*. He doesn't deal with the short story as such, but his comments on fiction are very relevant to the question of linearity. For him, fiction becomes one among a variety of human means for explaining experience—other important means being history and religion. These activities have in common the mission of giving a coherence beyond chronology to the log of "what happens." So, as he says elsewhere, "ends give meaning to events which, considered rawly as they occur in the middle, are either apparently random or have been wrongly or imperfectly explained [by other modes of interpretation]." [8]

Once we imagine that the world is sentenced to "end" for our sins—for our humanity, if you will—then, in relation to that outcome, all past, present, and tentative future existence can fall into place. We can say that narrative is explanation, and that behind every narrative there is some element related to the human set: some type. [9] The "type" that Kermode explores in his book is that of the Apocalypse, of "*the* end."

7. *Ibid.*, 180.
8. Kermode, "An Approach Through History," 29.
9. *Ibid.*, 24.

Novel-length narratives, with their tendency to deal in individual life-times, are but modeling themselves on this basic "type"—whatever the nature of the end they reach. Even the dynamics of drama conform to the pattern; Kermode redefines *peripeteia* as a reflection of the prediction-followed-by-"disconfirmation" syndrome, which is illustrated every time the world outlives its millennium.[10] But the fact that the world has not yet ended in no way damages the validity or lessens the power of that "sense of an ending." Its particular configuration of meaning endures as a pervasive "type" of explanation because it has great efficacy in organizing, integrating, and making sense of what falls to our lot. In any context, large or small, the postulation of an end retroactively posits a linear progression toward it—and that idea of progression-toward-an-end concentrates thought and regulates feeling whether or not the end really comes. We've already discussed the importance of linearity in short fiction. There we can endure the sequence, encounter the end—and survive it. All within the span of an hour or two.

Kermode explains that the religious model of the end of the world is but one of the typologies borrowed by fiction, but it is profoundly analogous to the traditional novelist's interest in the span of a life or the fate of a family. Eleanor N. Hutchens offers a significant corollary: "No matter what length of time the human action of a novel takes—whether it be a day or several generations—its paradigmatic structure is the normal human lifetime. Hence the most durable kind of novel is the *Bildungsroman*, which concentrates on the formative period of life, the youthful experience that sets the trajectory for the rest of the span."[11] Though her final image is linear, the concept of a lifetime can easily be adapted to the concept of a rhythm that contains all the moments pertinent to its fulfillment.

Genre

For David H. Richter, the problem of closure is a problem of genre.[12] He acknowledges the greater contemporary interest in "openness," but feels it is mistakenly based on some generalized sense of modern mal-

---

10. Kermode, *The Sense of an Ending*, 18, *et passim*.
11. Hutchens, "An Approach Through Time," 60.
12. Richter, *Fable's End*.

aise. The question is not what kind of century but what kind of fiction. For him, generic distinctions, a recognition of types of fictions, is a prerequisite to the proper understanding of types of endings and the proper evaluation of any particular ending. He is admittedly neo-Aristotelian. Relying on R. S. Crane, he distinguishes among three classes of fiction, and characterizes the way they may end.

Mimetic fictions may be divided into those with a "plot of action" and those with a "plot of character." In the first kind, "actions involve characters in unstable situations, and the removal of the instability and the consequent formation of a new stable situation provide us with the sense of an ending" (p. 166). In the second, or character-based kind, "a completed process of change in the moral [or other] character of the protagonist" achieves a new kind of completeness (pp. 5–6). Yet another category of fictions, those termed "rhetorical" rather than "mimetic," has normally a "plot of thought." These fictions end when the "inculcation of some doctrine or sentiment concerning the world external to the fiction" (p. 9) is achieved. Allegory, a special case of rhetorical fiction, is based on emblematic "interrelationships among [detachable] symbolic parts" (p. 15). Completeness here depends on fulfilling the independent logic of the ideas embodied in the fiction. And finally fable is another kind of rhetorical fiction, one "in which each detail of plot, characterization, and language is chosen in order to make us understand something in the external world . . . but in which the individual details generally do not have symbolic significance that can be detached from the fiction" (pp. 15–16). Completeness here "depends . . . on the choice of a denouement which most completely turns the emotional experience of the fictions into knowledge of the fictions' significance" (pp. 81–82).

Richter's categories are useful, especially as they allow him to apply to fiction Barbara H. Smith's distinction between "completeness" and "closure" in poetry.[13] Completeness comes about when we feel that the terms of a given kind of fiction have been met. Closure, on the other hand, may be imposed at any time, generally through the deployment of certain devices which we've learned to read as signals of "the end"— such as a return to the starting point, a marriage or a death, a crucial

13. Barbara H. Smith, *Poetic Closure*.

revelation, and so on. Richter is most helpful in pointing out that the principles of completeness may be different for different kinds of fiction, and that they need not coincide with principles of closure.

Normally, of course, completeness and closure do reinforce each other. But the fact that they are really independent variables can easily be overlooked and so lead to mistakes in critical judgment. Richter also reintroduces us to an ancient philosophical issue: do we recognize the genre we are reading by certain signals we've learned to identify after many exposures to the type; or do the genres correspond to innately differentiated modes of perception, so that we recognize what we are reading by the part of our mind that it taps? If there is such a thing as a "trained reader," he is probably someone whose experience has made him quick and certain in the reading of generic signals, including the principles of completeness. In the following discussion of linguistic paradigms, I will consider the possibility that the genres are, indeed, expressions of universal structures of mind. But before leaving Richter, I'd like to suggest that we regard his "completeness" as a subcategory of "closure" or "the sense of an ending."

Linguistics

Some very ingenious and suggestive work in the theory of fiction has been done by Victor Shklovsky and Tzvetan Todorov. Their work was described in the first chapter of this book but will be reviewed here from a slightly different angle. Simply speaking, the paradigmatic structure these men rely on is a linguistic one: the grammatical unit of the sentence. Let me spend a moment going over the parts of this model. Its basis is the kernel sentence, or the "proposition." To make a proposition, we need an agent about whom or about which something may be predicated. We specify an agent through some form of denomination, or naming—Robin, uncle, freedom—and we predicate something about it by describing a quality it has—naïve, wealthy, sudden—or by positing something it is or does—seeks, is shared, means. When we begin to combine these kernels, we perform certain operations on them, we make them undergo transformations. Thus, with a bit of amplification, we might say: Robin, a naïve young man from the country, seeks his fortune from an uncle in Boston; this uncle, a wealthy Tory, is shamed by a mob that contains his nephew; for the youth and for the nation, sudden freedom means the betrayal of the past. Now these three clauses are linked by implicit *and*'s. They form a series which could be extended indefinitely, for the structure of "linking" has a natural open-endedness.

But let's say we decide to arrange the clauses into some sort of hierarchy by framing or embedding two of them within the third. Depending upon which proposition we take to be the most important, we may come up with one of the following three possibilities:

1. Robin, a naïve young man from the country, seeks his fortune from an uncle who is a wealthy Tory, but, finding himself included in the mob that shames his uncle, he learns that sudden freedom means a betrayal of the past.
2. Robin's uncle, a wealthy Tory, intends to make the young man's fortune, but, having been shamed by a mob that includes his nephew, can only prove to him that sudden freedom means a betrayal of the past.
3. Sudden freedom, whether given to a naïve young man from the country or to a revolutionary mob, means a betrayal of the past and of its honored citizens.

The three sentences suggest three different kinds of discourse. The first is something like Hawthorne's "My Kinsman, Major Molineux." The second might be a story about the plight of a Tory in revolutionary Boston. The third could be an essay about the abuses of newfound freedom. But the sentences only hint at possibilities for development— possibilities which are infinitely varied. If we were actually to turn each of these sentences into a series of sentences, through an elaborate process of embedding new sentences into the series, as we have here embedded new kernels into the sentence, we would produce a sequence that could be a story.

The transformations we would perform at this supra-sentence level would be analogous to those we have performed at the sub-sentence level. Thus, instead of adding to the sentence a subordinating conjunction with its adverbial clause (*e.g.*, "because he felt so alienated from his home"), we might add to the story a flashback dream sequence showing Robin's family entering their home and shutting him out. Naturally, we do not suggest that Hawthorne did, in fact, follow such a procedure;

we merely use it as an analytic tool for uncovering and describing the elements of form we discern in the story.

What Todorov, building on Shklovsky, has done is to suggest a grammar for story modeled on the grammar for sentence. Subject and verb are protagonist and action; adjectivals are the modifying states and conditions that apply. Plots are analogous to grammatical transformations; most basically, structure is a function of coordination ("linking") or of subordination ("framing")—of "and" and "or" and "but," of "if" and "when" and "therefore." Finally, Todorov suggests that the minimal complete plot takes its protagonist from a state of equilibrium, through a state of disequilibrium, to a returned equilibrium. Any two parts of this sequence may yield a story. In effect, then, the adjectives of story describe the states of equilibrium *or* of disequilibrium; the verbs of story describe the passages from one state to another. Are we back again, then, to the classical model of developing action and denouement?

Perhaps not, if we think a while longer about the model of the sentence. In another chapter, I investigated the signs of fictionality in the story sentence and spoke about a "grammar of expectation" based on our built-in need to fill in the who that is or does, the being or doing that exists or happens, and the where-how-why and what-it's-like of the subject and verb combination. The way in which that grammar influences our "getting into story" is described in Chapter Three. But now I would like to return to a consideration of the sentence from a third perspective. My own view of story closure necessitates a return to this minimal unit of discourse—but a return that subordinates the linguistic to an organic typology.

Story as Rhythm

Periodicity

Most organic cycles—including the systole and diastole of the heartbeat, the inhaling and exhaling of air, and the rhythms of sex—consist of repeated, reciprocal acts. Yet if we look closely at one phase of a cycle, and ask "What is the movement that must be finished before it can be repeated?" we find something which begins and ends, something which has a period—a filling of the heart with blood, a filling of the lung with air, the stomach with food—even, in a manner of speaking, the filling of a day with waking, the filling of a life with living. In each case, we could say we have a resisting medium which yields to pressure until a limit is reached; sometimes that limit seems to be established by the finite tolerance of the medium; sometimes by the finite force of the pressure. Each of these periods may be cut short or varied in duration, but there is an expectancy time for each, and none may be prolonged beyond a limit peculiar to itself. How long can we go without breathing, eating, sleeping, dying?

How long can a sentence go without ending? Despite its variety of length, it, too, has its limits. That is why an experiment like Barthelme's "Sentence" is so interesting. By every device of enjambement, he draws out a string of words for almost eight pages, without a final stop, ending, finally, in mid-career. Has he proved that the sentence has no limit to its life? Just the reverse, it seems to me. He has merely put it on an artificial respirator of conjunctions and dashes. The reader will put in the periods. Though not everybody has a feel for punctuation, everybody has a feel for the implied limits of a sentence. Else language, as we know it, could not function. But let's look again at what the sentence is like. I've said it is composed of various syntactic and semantic features, various densities and intensities. These features interfere with the impetus to closure felt by all readers of English. In a way, then, the sentence is a resisting medium which yields to the pressure of our desire to assimilate, to "get the sense." I described several kinds of closure to account for the fact that we finish a sentence in several ways: by 1) simply reaching its end (physical closure), 2) gathering its meaning (immediate cognitive closure), and 3) appreciating its function within a discourse (deferred cognitive closure). Now, if a sentence may be viewed as a resisting medium through which we travel both mentally and physically, then perhaps we may think of the interferences as the resistance which defines the course of a movement. Rhythm is the shape of the movement. Rhythm is the shape of resistance overcome. In a millennium or a heartbeat or a sentence.

But how do we get from sentence to story? I've already shown how one can do it by means of an expanded "grammar of expectation." But now I'd like to shift the emphasis from a linguistic to an organic model. Let's go back to another everyday example of periodicity. Think of the times when we organize our body's force to achieve a particular impact—for example hitting a golf ball. As we walk to our place, we may be preparing in subtle ways for what is to come, but for the most part our body is taking care of itself, and if we back up far enough in time, we can watch this body scratching its knee and talking to Mrs. Jones about the weather. After the teeing off, we may see this body throw up its hands, rub its shoulders, bask in praise, or just walk away. What it does before and what it does after is relatively random, but what it does during those few moments from the positioning of feet, through the practiced swing, through the feel of impact, through the torque of completion—well, that is a unified movement controlled by vectors of force aimed at a point of impact and then fulfilling the idea of its curve.[14] This unified movement represents a period of end-directed, concentrated energy, preceded and followed by states of less intense, less precisely directed, and far more random expenditures of energy. It also resembles those biological cycles we've noted; it is the result of a staggeringly complex system of constraints—here most obviously the air resistance, length of arm, strength, aim, and skill of the golfer. A story, too, as I've said, is what is left when a variety of constraints are artfully conceived, met, exploited. But here, too, as in the analogies from organic experience, the result has a staggeringly simple wholeness. Liberally interpreted, Poe's effect is either the ball squarely hit, or the swing so finely made that the ball is unnecessary. So let us say, then, that the writer of fiction walks up to the tee; by a happy stroke of inspiration (if you like) or by the most painstaking and tortuous effort, he creates out of the totality of his experience, and by the artfully constrained use of verbal symbols, a rhythm of purposely arranged information. The reader then undergoes, within the totality of *his* experience, a curve of intensified responding. He experiences what the author has created: density, intensity, linearity, spatiality—in short the reality warp of the story. He experiences the rhythm of the story. And insofar as that rhythm interferes with and competes with other rhythms in his life, his heightened and specialized attention, his response to the story creates a reality warp within his own experience. It is a period of active reorientation—concentrated and demanding.

Starting again with a consideration of how a story comes into being, let me now suggest a correlation between organic periods of low-to-

14. This illustration was suggested to me by Paul Byron Diehl, at The University of Iowa.

high and high-to-low levels of energy/organization, and a movement into and out of coherent discourse.

IN AND OUT OF COHERENCE
(with apologies to Gogol)

STASIS (no information; tautology)

> he
> he is he
> he

RHYTHM
   AS REPETITION
       (minimal semantic information)   he he he he he he he he
       (minimal syntactic information)   he wanted, he wanted, he wanted,

   AS CLOSURE   He wanted an overcoat.

DISCOURSE (connected propositions)
   Modes: exposition
           description
           argument
           NARRATION   He wanted an overcoat. He got it. He lost it.

> The variety of possibilities are infinite, and include his losing and then regaining the overcoat, his getting and then not wanting the overcoat, his wondering why he wanted the overcoat, his getting it and then wanting an umbrella and galoshes, etc., etc.

EXPANSION (embedded information)   He went into the store, which was filled with rows of bodiless coats.

SEQUENCE (information added by the same generative principle, *e.g.*, chronology)   He bought the overcoat. He put it on. He walked out the door.

SUCCESSION (no information; nonsense)   he overcoat the wore put . . .

This diagram may suggest that even minimally coherent discourse is poised between two poles of nonsense—unconstrained synchronicity and unconstrained diachronicity. Remembering that linearity is the result of urging X_1,X_1,X_1,X_1 into the sequence X_1,X_2,X_3,X_4, and remembering that plot is the effect of closing off that sequence at some necessary X_n, we might see how easily story fits into the diagram. Story, as a specially constrained sort of discourse, is also composed of incremental sense—even if it is only the sense of deliberate nonsense. Story, too, is a complexly interlinked sequence of periods. But from the point of view of sophisticated reading, what kind of experience is provided?

At this point we need to make a further distinction between fiction and other kinds of discourse by saying that it creates a surrogate environment for the reader; whether or not it tries to imitate a "real" one, it certainly aims to displace a "real" one. Temporarily. As my example of narrative discourse in the diagram, I used a synopsis of Gogol's famous short story "The Overcoat." But I didn't give you the world of the story, the world that *is* the story. For our experience of this fictional environment, of this reality warp, is an experience of all the words, of all the sentences, that come between the start and the stop. They are what keep us from skipping to the end—to get easy closure. Our experience of reading a story is an experience of meeting resistance. That resistance requires a complex and extended act of assimilation. And here I am back to the golf swing. Rhythm is the shape of resistance overcome. Rhythm is the shape of the story. To read the story is to experience the rhythm.

Closure

It has always been clear that a short story's chief difference from longer fiction has to do with the aesthetics of brevity, but no one has gone very far toward explaining Poe's original conception of the "unity of expression." I'd simply point to the function of closure in defining a rhythm. Periodicity, in biology, history, and aesthetics, is engendered by the notion of closure—not the other way around. Short fiction, it has been said, is the most "end-conscious" of forms. Readers of short fiction are the most end-conscious of readers. Perhaps the reason is that the end is generally not given before they have had time to be curious about it, nor is it then withheld for very long.

Put another way, the period of the short story may approximate a shorter paradigm than that of other fiction. Earlier I mentioned Eleanor Hutchens' guess that the paradigmatic period of the novel is the human life-span. My guess is that the paradigmatic time span of the short story is twenty-four hours. Of course not all stories keep to this period, any more than all novels keep to the period of the lifetime; nevertheless, a surprising number do, and in any case it is a useful norm. The psychological and sensory predominance of the diurnal cycle, the simple peripeteia of day-into-night or night-into-day, the highly determined singularity of each day (named and numbered as it is), the space it offers for the expression of each or any of the basic human drives, and finally the natural suitability of the day as a synecdoche for the life—all these features of the twenty-four-hour period make it a likely analogue for the "felt time" of a story. It may even promote our understanding of the rhythmic period of stories that deal with only a moment's time or with a good many years.

Even more helpful than the notion of a paradigmatic time period may be the notion of a paradigmatic verb for the sentence of the story. Do you recall the diagram illustrating the movement into and out of coherent sense? There I used a synopsis of "The Overcoat" to stand as an example of a particular story sentence. But it would be better if we could find a sentence which would, with appropriate modifications, fit any story. All along I've been describing stories as invitations to enter a reality warp created by the author. Usually the story depicts a character undergoing a reality warp within his own experience. For the reader, the reality warp is always an experience of reading. For the character, it may be the experience of losing or gaining an ideal or a wife, a coat or a conviction. By definition, reality warps cause disorientation. This whole book is about the way readers adapt to the story's world or come to an understanding of it; the stories themselves are about how the characters experience heightened or significant portions of their lives. Are they losing their bearings? Are they "homing in"? If we interpret "home" in the broadest sense, as the place where our reality is so comfortable and well known—so unwarped—that we can manage in the dark, then perhaps we can say that every story shows us someone either coming home or leaving home. Though there is nothing fixed about these directions, many stories give us a character moving toward knowledge of his past, his true self, his real fate. These movements might be called homecomings. Movements into the future, the unknown, some other, as yet un-defined self—these might well be home-leavings. A story may show one direction more prominently than the other, or it may give us a paradox, a combination of both. In deciding how the paradigm sentence applies, we may simply be confirming or testing what we feel in other ways, know in other terms.

I must again stress that I am not referring to plot in the usual sense, but to the presentation of selected information. I'm talking about the dynamics of the interaction between the accumulating sentences and the assimilating mind. Remembering the typologies of closure reviewed at the beginning of this chapter, I am tempted to add that, for both author and reader, the impetus to closure on the story level is really an internalized expectation of patterns we've noted in life: problems followed by solutions, meetings followed by partings, the unknown yielding to the known, and the known giving way to the unknown. All can be described as ways of either coming home or leaving home.

Here I might mention how eager the New Critics have been to abstract their "unities" from these patterns of closure—especially the linear and spatial figures of repetition, divergence, and convergence. But the fact is that the artist's observation may yield patterns of infinite variety and complexity, including the absence of any (apparent) pattern at all. Hence, the narrative discourse we read has a potentially infinite variety of sequences, including some which are imitations of chaos. Let William Carlos Williams have his "deformities," Joyce Carol Oates her "dreams," Welty her "mysteries," and Gordimer her "flashes of fireflies." All can be dealt with by the terms of the reality warp. Each can make its own rhythm in fiction.

Endings

Of course sometimes we are displeased with the ending of a story. Every schoolchild used to be familiar with such stories as "The Lady or the Tiger?" by Frank Stockton, "The Gift of the Magi," by O. Henry, and "The Necklace" by de Maupassant. Each is an example of the kind of story that seems to be written merely for the shock of its very last sentence. The story is a device for conveying us to the conclusion with the least interference along the way and the maximum impact at the end. However, it is worth noting, as Ian Reid wisely does, that such stories are not categorically "bad." They are in critical disrepute because they exhibit a simple notion of plot that can easily become simplistic, formulaic, and trivial. Reid, in his short treatise on the short story, distinguishes between an O. Henry story which is merely a gimmick and a de Maupassant story in which the surprise ending "jolts us into perceiving something fundamental about what we have been reading."[15]

There are times, too, when we have the opposite problem—not too much ending but too little. We say that it "shouldn't have ended there" or that it "doesn't really have an ending at all." Again, the reason may be that the story is a poor one. Or it may be that we haven't had enough experience with the kind of stimuli provided to be able to take in the meaning at the rate the author expects of us. He's done; we're not. And what about the great modern discovery of the "open" short story? As I've mentioned before, the closing off of possibilities is not the only way in which a story may grant that equilibrium of information and assimilation. The reader may also be brought to an awareness of ramified implications. We do not need to feel that the obscure has been made plain. Mystery is not confusion; it is the outline of wonder. A story can lead us into dismay and yet make us feel that we've assimilated our information in a satisfactory—though difficult—way. The deferred cognitive closure may be by far the richest part of the experience. By contrast, the discovery that "the point is pointlessness" may be one of the easier kinds of equilibrium to reach. Perhaps that is why so many stories of that kind now seem, paradoxically, to shut off insight rather than to open it up.

Remember, too, that what happens at the end of a story is not necessarily (though it usually is) marked by devices of closure—the mystery solved, the goal won or lost, the disparate joined, or the joined divided. Rhythm as closure demands only that a limit of tolerance be reached. A sigh or a gasp. And so it can happen explosively, like the burst at the end of a deep inhalation. "The Pit and the Pendulum" ends like that, and so do some stories by Joyce Carol Oates. Or it can happen gently, like the quiet end of a long exhalation. "The Lady with the Dog" ends like that, and so do many stories by Raymond Carver. If I wanted other examples, I would probably ask Randall Jarrell, for among the critics who have been most helpful to me, he has gone farthest toward an organic

15. Reid, *The Short Story*, 62.

theory of the form. His discussion of endings might have been very much like mine, had he pressed home his analogies:

> In stories-in-which-everything-is-a-happening each event is charged and about to be further charged, so that the narrative may at any moment reach a point of unbearable significance, and disintegrate into energy. In stories-in-which-nothing-happens even the climax or denouement is liable to lose what charge it has, and to become simply one more portion of the lyric, humorous, or contemplative continuum of the story. . . .
>
> One of these extremes of narrative will remind us of the state of minimum excitation which the organism tries to re-establish—of the baby asleep, a lyric smile on his lips; the other extreme resembles the processes of continually increased excitation found in sex and play.[16]

We'll keep on reading if our appetite stays ahead of our ability to assimilate, so that, in our reading, even more intensely than in our living, we experience the impetus to closure. Ideally there is a point at which the need to have more and the need to assimilate reach equilibrium. Perhaps we never hit the point exactly, for this may be one of those balances of nature which are always in the process of righting themselves. But the art of the short story is manifest in the guiding of the balance arm to rest—briefly, illusorily—for the sake of our need.

The Last Rip, the Last Wave, and the Last "No"

In the previous chapters we entered and got well on our way through "Rip Van Winkle," "The Open Boat," and "Flowering Judas." Breaking up these texts is of course a violation of the reading experience, particularly harmful to a theory based on the continuity of that experience. But my excerpts are meant only to recall to you the entire text, and to serve as points of reference for my own exposition. I will, therefore, ask you to keep in mind all that precedes these final sentences from the stories by Irving, Crane, and Porter:

> —Even to this day they never hear a thunderstorm of a summer afternoon about the Kaatskill, but they say Hendrick Hudson and his crew are at their game of nine-pins; and it is a common wish of all hen-pecked husbands in the neighborhood, when life hangs heavy on their hands, that they might have a quieting draught out of Rip Van Winkle's flagon.[17]
>
> *

16. Jarrell, "Stories," 43.
17. Irving, "Rip Van Winkle," 41.

When it came night, the white waves paced to and fro in the moonlight, and the wind brought the sound of the great sea's voice to the men on the shore, and they felt that they could then be interpreters.[18]

*

Laura cried No! and at the sound of her own voice, she awoke trembling, and was afraid to sleep again.[19]

Taken in isolation, the first two sentences announce their finality. They do so through what Barbara H. Smith would call signals of closure: "even to this day" (implying a previously explained condition of the old days), "all hen-pecked husbands" (implying a summary of inductive evidence), and "then" (in the sense of "now at last," implying a final result). The sentence from "Flowering Judas," on the other hand, contains no obvious signals of closure; those that are in fact there are perceivable only in terms of, and in the context of, this particular story.

So let us begin with the end of "Rip Van Winkle." It is a dense and leisurely sentence, clearly offered by a narrator whose involvement in Rip's experience is detached, amused, perhaps wry, benevolent—in short, characteristic of Irving via Crayon via Knickerbocker. Rip has dissolved into the voice of his amiable historian, for whom the "they" of the townspeople has taken precedence over the "he" of the hero. Rip himself is displaced by the legend he has sponsored; what happens in the sentence is only an emblem of what has happened in the story. For there Rip sacrifices twenty years, or the prime of his life, for a bit of immortal folklore. "What great artist wouldn't?" you say. "What great artist hasn't," says Irving.

From the point of view of its linearity, "Rip Van Winkle" ends with the last stage in the hero's transformations. Rip_1 has become the Rip_n who is a wishfully envied old man, almost a legend himself. We sense this as we achieve cognitive closure for the story. But from the point of view of its spatiality, the story is an emblem of the artist's displacement in a society of practical "doers." If every man is married to the world, every artist is a hen-pecked husband. That's what we might be considering as we move through stages of deferred cognitive closure. We could graph the line of the story; we could see its end as the fulfillment of an American millennium (the pre-Revolutionary era), the completion of a

18. Crane, "The Open Boat," 92.
19. Porter, "Flowering Judas," 102.

sentence about where Rip went, or the quiet exhalation of the narrator's breath. With a very great story, there will always be several typologies that will seem to fit. Feeling the rhythm of the story is feeling the aptness of those that do fit. For me, this is a story of the homecoming type: we're taken home to our past, as Rip is taken home to himself. All the effects of density, intensity, linearity, and spatiality—all tell us what kind of homecoming this is. When we reach that knowledge, we've completed the rhythm. We've ended the story.

Before we get to the end of Crane's story, we must pass through its seven numbered divisions. These are seven waves that move us toward the beach at the end. Earlier I described the sequences of error-and-correction, the perceptual rhythms which, like blending waves, make a single rising tide. What is the meaning of the slicing fin? The speck on the shore? That star up above? The oiler's death? The story is a dramatized act of interpretation. By the end, the survivors feel that they, by virtue of what they've been through, can now interpret the voice of the sea. Perhaps what they are interpreting are the ways of Nature toward man. Justifying them is out of the question.

How many thousands of students have finished this story only to face a command to explain it. They are being asked to give public, discursive form to deferred cognitive closure. Out of habit or desperation, they are likely to plug in terms like *theme* and *setting* and *character*. But if the end of this story is thought of as the closure which defines its period, if that period is described as the rhythm created by the movement through artfully monitored features of density, intensity, linearity, and spatiality—then the chances are much greater that the reader's act of interpretation will be an organic continuation of his act of reading.

And what are we to do with the ending Porter gives us? Laura, we know, has been crying "no!" all through the story. But this is the first time she hears it aloud. We've seen her be unaware of, inwardly repelled by, or even naughtily amused by the love she arouses in others. She is a self-imposed exile from passion. Yet she lives in terror of the breakdown of her defenses. Now she has just allowed, in fact aided, a young man to kill himself. Apparently, for him, the pain of not living fully was greater than the pain of not living at all. At any rate, Laura, in her aloofness, has given him the narcotic of indifference rather than the nourishment of love.

Closure here, as often in primarily spatial stories, is a function of converging references. The overall design becomes clear as separate strands of imagery either intersect or reveal their parallelism. In her waking hours, earlier that same day, Laura left her house and passed through the streets of the town where she has kept herself a stranger. She visited the prison and discovered that Eugenio, using the narcotic she had given him, was committing suicide that day. In the dream, Eugenio, now a spirit from the world of the dead, leads her from her house into a sterile landscape. Now *she* begs for human contact, the touch of his hand; now *he* withholds it, eluding her grasp. He calls *her* the "poor prisoner," and, in cruel imitation of her own behavior, gives her, instead of his hand, the bleeding flowers of the Judas tree. "Take and eat," he says. Laura's Catholicism, stifled in her waking life, haunts her here in this gruesome communion. Flowers, the gift of love from her pupils, and her own perversion of the Lord's Prayer,[20] all the denials of her life merge with the image of betrayal. Eugenio is the Christ whom she has denied and "cannibalized" through her willingness to let others do her living for her. When the full implication of the blasphemy is stated, "Laura cried No!"

Other critics have noted the strange shift in tense here. The persistent present tense, used throughout as the medium of Laura's somnambulent life, is here punctured by a fixed point in time. Laura has been jerked awake. If, in addition to its spatial design, the story has a potent linear progression, it may be revealed only in these very last words. For Laura's waking life has been in fact dreamlike; she has moved as though in a trance through a world kept sterile by her "notorious virginity," her unyielding breasts (swollen, "like a nursing mother's," with ungiven milk). Now this waking trance has culminated in an actual dream. Paradoxically, the dream has shown the "reality" of her way of life. She wakes. She cries "No!" This time to the dream. And she stays awake, now, out of fear.

Like Christ addressing the sinful, Eugenio has commanded Laura to "get up . . . and follow me." He has told her to "come out of your sleep, out of your bed, out of this strange house." But this is her own house, the house of her self-containment. Is he implying that her true home,

---

20. Discussed in Chapter Four herein.

her true self, is elsewhere? Let us suppose that the dream does indeed reach her bed in the heart of her house, and it calls upon her to leave that sleep, that bed, that house, that self. What then? In the past, Laura has come close to self-criticism, close to leaving her false home: but "still she sits quietly, she does not run. Where could she go?" And again: "I must run while there is time. But she does not go." Will she go now?

In effect, we are asking what is the relationship of this final "no" to the others. Is she still afraid to admit the truth, and therefore rejecting the dream's assault? If so, this "no" is just like the rest. It is one more "no" in the series. But is she perhaps frightened more deeply than before? Could she be saying "no" to the person she now sees she's become? If so, this "no" *is* different. It is a crucial "no₂".

Unlike "Rip Van Winkle" and "The Open Boat," this story is not obviously a homecoming. It is a tensely, beautifully achieved potential for leaving a false home. Poised between a dead series and a jumbled chaos, caught between a gasp and a sigh, this story is holding its breath.

CHAPTER SIX

The Classics

• • •

In this chapter I would like to invite you back to the nineteenth century, when the American art story came into being. Its "origins, growth, and development" have been traced often enough, but usually in relation to the larger literary and cultural movements shaping the century.[1] Since my interest is not historical but generically aesthetic, I will forego the survey and concentrate on two examples which pose significant but widely differing problems to the short story critic.

Perhaps it is true that we remember stories the way we remember dreams, either vividly and holistically, or subliminally—awaiting some cue that will call up the whole—or only by inference from the sweat on the brow, the book on the shelf. I doubt that there is a student of American literary history who would not feel he should remember "Roger Malvin's Burial." If, for a split second, he were to confuse it with Poe's "Premature Burial," he'd soon realize that both stories evoke the horror of meeting a slow death while one's eyes are open but nobody's there. Still, that is not the image apt to linger in the minds of those who have read Hawthorne's story. More likely they will recall a tableau in the forest with a father gazing down at the son he has killed. It is an indelible scene, one that comes to mind with the clarity of déjà vu. It is as hard to forget as a recurring nightmare. On the other hand, I doubt whether many of these same readers have ever heard of "Athénaïse." They might recognize the name of the author, Kate Chopin; they might very well know her novel *The Awakening*—for it was resurrected in the 1950s and

1. See, for example: Pattee, *The Development of the American Short Story*; Peden, *The American Short Story*; Ross, *The American Short Story*; West, *The Short Story in America, 1900–1950*.

is now firmly established as a masterpiece of prose lyricism, psychological insight, and (unfortunately for the author) premature realism—especially in the realm of female sensuality. But how does the story "Athénaïse" begin, move, and end? Few would blush for not knowing. Yet this story has been called a perfect achievement, a brilliant example of the local color subgenre transcended through wisdom and artistry. It is as hard to forget as a recurring daydream.

Of course Chopin is a lesser writer than Hawthorne, as well as a more recent addition to the canon. These factors certainly influence the kind and degree of attention given to their stories. But it is also interesting to note that "Roger Malvin's Burial" has generated an unusual number of contradictory interpretations, while "Athénaïse" has received very few but relatively uniform treatments. I would say that both of these situations are, in different ways, "problems" inherited by American short story critics. Let me take them up one at a time.

"Roger Malvin's Burial," by Nathaniel Hawthorne

The Story

Hawthorne begins with a brief exposition about a well-known battle between New England settlers and the Indians they've displaced. It is a costly victory for the colonists, whose deeds will be remembered in tales of "Lovell's Fight." On the way home from the encounter, two stragglers—a badly injured young man and his fatally wounded older comrade—come to rest under an oak tree; the young man, Reuben Bourne, is the intended son-in-law of the older man, Roger Malvin, and is willing to sacrifice his own life to remain by the dying man's side. After much indecision, Reuben is persuaded to seek his own safety and happiness; he does, however, promise to return to bury Roger Malvin according to civilized custom. Days later, having lost his way, Reuben is found by a search party, is brought back to the village, and is tended by Roger Malvin's daughter. Dorcas jumps to the conclusion that her suitor had in fact stayed to perform her father's burial, and spreads the word of his heroic deed; shamed, Reuben never corrects the presumption, leads a luckless and bitter life under the shadow of the lie, and eventually decides to look for new fortune in the wilderness. Accompanied by his wife and sixteen-year-old son (whom he loves as the reincarnation of his better self, his redemption in posterity), Reuben finds his steps mysteriously guided back to the part of the forest where he had abandoned his friend; while both Reuben and his son are foraging for deer, the father shoots at a movement in the underbrush and arrives to find the son dead on the very spot where his grandfather's bones are moldering. The final tableau depicts the mother grieving over the bodies of her son and father, while her husband meditates upon the scene, is moved to tears, and—for the first time in years—to prayer; his "sin" is "expiated."

When the reader of this story achieves physical closure and puts down the book, it is very likely that cognitive closure—both immediate and deferred—will be some while in coming. For can the murder of a son be anything but a crime worse than the one it redeems? And if the expiation is obscure, so, too, is the guilt. What sin, if any, did Reuben commit? Should he have stayed in the forest to die? Is there a higher law than those that excused him for leaving? Or was he in the right when he left, but in the wrong when he failed to return? Possibly it was not any of these things he might have done and didn't, but the one thing he shouldn't have done—and did: conceal the truth. And in any case, how are we to take a story that leads off with a historical footnote?

The Critics

Scholars have found documented records of Lovell's—or Lovewell's—Fight, as well as a ballad describing the grieving separation of the wounded stragglers from their dying comrades.[2] From another source comes the mention of a handkerchief tied to a tree as a marker for a returning search party, and a request from a dying man that his companion brace him up against a support.[3] It would seem beyond doubt that the story is meant to have some connection with historical fact.

Other critics have looked for the deeper cultural roots of the story. Parallels have been suggested between the story's seasonal/burial motifs and the Roman *Lemuria*,[4] but by far the most interesting allusions are biblical. "Reuben," brother of Joseph, was a breaker of promises: he vowed to return to save the boy from the pit into which his brothers

2. Orians, "The Source of 'Roger Malvin's Burial.'"
3. Lovejoy, "Lovewell's Fight and Hawthorne's 'Roger Malvin's Burial.'"
4. McCullen, "Ancient Rites for the Dead and Hawthorne's 'Roger Malvin's Burial.'"

had cast him—but he didn't come back. "Cyrus," on the other hand, was a biblical hero. He was the redeemer of Israel, a man who could make water gush from rocks, even as the tears are made to gush from Reuben's stony heart at the end of Hawthorne's story. Remembering the biblical Cyrus helps us to see Reuben Bourne's son as his hope for the future, for the dynasty—the new Israel—he might have founded had his child lived to be the father of sons. Also, implicit in this personal posterity is the future of New England, which Lovewell's Fight was supposed to ensure.[5] Finally, there may be another biblical allusion, much more indirect, to the woman in St. Luke who served the Devil for eighteen long years—the very period for which Reuben is exiled from hope.[6] Whether or not one takes this last analogue seriously, there is something compelling in the notion of a spanned absence from God.

During the sixties and early seventies, there appeared a number of articles and portions of books attempting to locate Reuben's guilt and to explain its effects. Ultimately, these critics faced each other over the body of Cyrus. For Agnes M. Donohue, his death makes sense if one views the action of the story as a Calvinist paradigm.[7] Reuben is an Everyman whose God-the-Father "wiles" him into choosing life and happiness at the expense of his soul. In punishment, Reuben must pay the price of discovering "life" to be "death," or, in other words, a death-in-life caused by human fallibility. He must also pay an emblematic price; for failing to be a saint, he must lose the best dream of mankind—nothing less than an innocently Adamic future for the Puritan "saints." Such a reading of the story is full of suggestion, if one wishes to see Hawthorne primarily in religio-historical terms. But it still results in the dehumanization of Cyrus. His death becomes a foregone conclusion, a sacrifice entailed upon him by the onerous humanity of his elders. But surely Donohue is right about the archetype: somehow, Cyrus is to be associated with the prelapsarian America forfeited by Everyman's fall in New England. Other interpretations are possible, but none is more basic.

No doubt the most influential approach to the story is the one taken by Frederick Crews.[8] In a thorough review of the criticism up to his

5. Thompson, "The Biblical Sources of Hawthorne's 'Roger Malvin's Burial.'"
6. White, "Hawthorne's Eighteen-Year Cycle."
7. Donohue, "'From Whose Bourne No Traveller Returns.'"
8. Crews, "The Logic of Compulsion in 'Roger Malvin's Burial.'"

time, Crews points out that the emphases have been on sources, symbols, and moral/ethical themes. He wishes to emphasize the psychology of motivation. Reuben, subconsciously realizing that his desire for happiness involves a wish for the death of Roger as father figure, feels guilty for leaving the old man to die; as the fruit of that happiness—Cyrus—matures, Reuben sees this son as the incarnation of the guilty part of himself, the part that must eventually be destroyed. Thus, in the Freudian sense, he does indeed have "unconscious knowledge" of where he is in the forest; what guides him through the action of the last phase of the story is a "logic of compulsion." Reuben is too practiced a woodsman, and, ironically, too loving a father, to be shooting so carelessly. He knows, at some deep level, that he's aimed at his son; it is a necessary atonement. Neither God nor man requires, or would ever condone, this logic; it is predicated on the deepest Oedipal configuration of instincts, moving the mind, the feet, and the hand to their deed. Yet, according to this reading, hasn't Reuben moved from a condition of imagined guilt to one of very real guilt? If he has expiated the death wish he visited on Malvin, how is he going to expiate the death blow he's given to Cyrus? Does Hawthorne often leave so much guilt in the balance—unaccounted for, left over, forgotten? Don't we still wonder how this story can end as it does, with such calm resolution?

There are other ways of looking at Reuben. Gloria Erlich sees him as a stand-in for Hawthorne, who, through this character, is reliving a childhood fantasy of revenge against a surrogate father, a maternal uncle whose initials are the same as Roger Malvin's.[9] These old men demand gratitude, they impose obligations. Killing Cyrus is a way of punishing them—for we recall that the boy is not only Malvin's grandson (on the mother's side) but also his young incarnation. Yet Reuben suffers, too. This is Hawthorne's way of atoning for his fantasy. But another critic reminds us that Roger Malvin does, indeed, get "buried." Those leaves fall upon grandson and grandsire, covering them both. Thus the boy's death has this significance, too: it fulfills the vow all the fuss was about.[10] For yet another reader, the tragedy has yet another dimension. According to Dieter Schulz, Reuben blights his own life by committing the cardinal sin of Romanticism; by giving in to a dangerous solipsism, by failing to check his imagination against common

9. Erlich, "Guilt and Expiation in 'Roger Malvin's Burial.'"
10. Robillard, "Hawthorne's 'Roger Malvin's Burial.'"

sense, he loses perspective, succumbs to an interior guilt, and suffers— as usual in Hawthorne—a dislocation from society.[11] Perhaps here the death of Cyrus is finally accounted for in terms of its inadmissibility: only a father completely lost to reason and good sense could accept an act for which no justification—moral or intellectual—exists.

There are, of course, other perspectives. To one critic Reuben is another Young Goodman Brown, foolishly warring with darkness.[12] For another, Jack Kligerman, he is a captive of grammar. Time and again he is acted upon by nominal abstractions; he is passive under the assault of nouns which name psychological forces. Kligerman believes that Cyrus' death is accidental, but that, in the act of accepting responsibility for it, Reuben for the first time takes moral charge of his life. He takes over the nominative function in the sentence of his life.[13] But Cyrus remains in the accusative.

By reviewing these interpretations of the story, I've tried to show the extent to which critical opinion has agreed on the power and importance of the story, yet divided on matters of substance. There has been, for example, no finally satisfying way of accounting for 1) the relevance of the introductory historical note, 2) the kinds and occasions of guilt within Reuben, and 3) the meaning of Cyrus' death. So much diversity of opinion suggests that the story is both rich and ambiguous. I've no hope of resolving the differences nor of transcending them neatly or definitively. Rather, I want to see whether just such a "problem" story as this one—yielding so much to so many kinds of traditional criticism (source-study, historical, biographical, Freudian, New Critical)—will give up yet something more to a study based on an aesthetic of short fiction.

Kronos and Kairos

How do we begin, move through, and get out of this story? What can we learn from density and intensity, from linearity and spatiality,

11. Schulz, "Imagination and Self-Imprisonment: The Ending of 'Roger Malvin's Burial.'"

12. Liebman, "'Roger Malvin's Burial.'"

13. Kligerman, "A Stylistic Approach to Hawthorne's 'Roger Malvin's Burial.'" One problem with Kligerman's analysis is that he hasn't put his discussion in the context of nineteenth-century norms, or even of habitual practice within Hawthorne's work as a whole.

from the reality warp of this story? We start by making a chronological adjustment. After we sit down to read, we lean back in time.

> One of the few incidents of Indian warfare, naturally susceptible of the moonlight of romance, was that expedition, undertaken, for the defense of the frontiers, in the year 1725, which resulted in the well-remembered "Lovell's Fight." Imagination, by casting certain circumstances judicially into the shade, may see much to admire in the heroism of a little band, who gave battle to twice their number in the heart of the enemy's country. The open bravery displayed by both parties was in accordance with civilized ideas of valor, and chivalry itself might not blush to record the deeds of one or two individuals. The battle, though so fatal to those who fought, was not unfortunate in its consequences to the country; for it broke the strength of a tribe, and conduced to the peace which subsisted during several ensuing years. History and tradition are unusually minute in their memorials of this affair; and the captain of a scouting party of frontier-men has acquired as actual a military renown, as many a victorious leader of thousands. Some of the incidents contained in the following pages will be recognized, not withstanding the substitution of fictitious names, by such as have heard, from old men's lips, the fate of the few combatants who were in a condition to retreat, after "Lovell's Fight." [14]

We have been rhetorically maneuvered into identifying ourselves with those likely to have heard the old men; we join those for whom the tag "Lovell's Fight" calls up a "well-remembered" legend. Yet the chances are that we really aren't members of that group, and Hawthorne knows it. The chances are that we may hear (with one ear, as it were) something like this: to preserve the existence of a European colony in the New World, a small group of settlers do battle with the "enemy" (whose country has been invaded to its "heart," but who nevertheless have "civilized ideas of valor"); the white men are sacrificed to the future of their community, and are rewarded with a glorified renown. Of course I have been giving this summary a modernized slant, but we do seem invited to be critical. After all, Hawthorne tells us that we can admire Lovell and his men only "by casting certain circumstances judicially into the shade." Among those circumstances may be the fact that the honor of the "expedition" is clearly in doubt. So, interesting as it is to know that there really was a "Lovewell" and that Hawthorne knew details of his "Fight," I think this information is of secondary importance. What mat-

---

14. Hawthorne, "Roger Malvin's Burial," 337–38.

ters is the process by which a certain kind of imagination—the kind that creates a legend—serves communal self-interest. Hawthorne brilliantly prepares for a further step in the process; using his kind of imagination, he is now going to tell a story that calls us back to a realization of moral truths and personal prices. I believe the opening of the story works upon us to this end whether or not we know the truth about Lovell.

Almost every critic of the story does agree that Malvin is a surrogate for Reuben's father. He is almost a surrogate for the community itself, for he is one of its veteran defenders and largest shareholders (able to bequeath a farm "under older cultivation, larger, and better stocked than most of the frontier establishments"); furthermore, as the father of Dorcas, he can also bestow the opportunity for family growth and continuity. Perhaps more importantly, he has the experienced breadth of mind which enables him to lay before Reuben what would be called, in presently fashionable parlance, a convincing "scenario" for the future.

We first see the two men resting on a bed of leaves; Reuben is asleep, controlled by his "dreaming fancy"; Malvin, however, is wide awake in every sense. He is fully aware of his true situation, his imminent death. After Reuben is jolted from his dream by its very violence, Malvin begins the process of convincing him to leave. To this end he does beguile Reuben—perhaps deliberately to tempt a soul to ruin, perhaps selflessly to save another's life, or maybe somehow to ease impending death. He leads Reuben's sanguine imagination through an alternative plot—a rescue followed by a happy marriage and a long posterity. For final emphasis, he uses the example of his own experience of twenty years before. He poses an analogy. In that other case, *he* left a wounded friend who was later rescued and revived.

In his higher wisdom, Malvin "secretly acknowledge[s] the wide dissimilarity between the two cases." Yet the differences do not appear obvious in Malvin's telling of the tale. Reuben fails to see them. Perhaps we do, too, unless we are more astute, more dispassionate, more careful than Reuben. Is that too much to ask of a reader? Isn't that just what Hawthorne asks of us in that strange introductory paragraph? Now, in the case of Malvin's own tale, we may guess that "certain circumstances" have again been "judicially [cast] into the shade." We can bring to light at least two: In the analogy, Malvin's friend was a contemporary of his, not a much older man; the chances for his survival were reasonably good, whereas the chances for Malvin are nil. These differences are crucial to the ethical point. But Malvin suppresses them and Reuben does not try too hard to uncover them. To each the tale is a means to an end, and that end is the preservation of life—personal, familial, societal—and the making of "history."

Let me now remind you of ideas introduced in the earlier chapters. We are "in" the story the moment we cross the ontological gap. We are "in" when we adjust to the reality warp. That adjustment is not simply an orientation in history; it is a matter of responding to density and intensity. To the modern ear, the language of this story seems formally genteel, not ungraceful, but stately rather than fluent, turning magisterially on a semicolon, collecting its clauses, rarely yielding its period in short of fifteen words and often waiting for fifty. It is a dense style, though depending heavily on the compounding of simple clauses. Rarely does a nominative absolute turn up, and almost never a fragment. The pace is measured, inexorable. Yet the syntax readily admits the inclusion of qualification, of multiple side-lights on the main proposition. Reading these sentences is no easy route to closure. One is drawn in and around and beneath the statements. Intensity, in the sense we have used it before, is not easy to describe. There is a lexicon of "loaded" words (*e.g.*, "heart," "sympathy," "chain," "secret," "cover," "conceal," "serpent," "wither," "sunlight," "moonlight," etc.). For the most part, this lexicon is stable throughout the Hawthorne canon. But some words—like "father," "son," and "vow"—acquire, within this story especially, a glow of moral significance that heats them with meaning. As we'll see later, words like "youthful" and "adventurous" have an unusually high valence. Thus, intensity here is felt in terms of large thematic endowments given to certain words, rather than in terms of the semantic content of the words themselves. It's remarkable, indeed, that the death of Cyrus is accomplished without a word of blood. In short, the density and intensity of the story's sentences make us come to know their world through careful, conscientious, morally sensitive steps. In this story, people jump to conclusions with disastrous results; however, the reading experience is so conditioned that our own conclusions are difficult to reach. Hence the diversity of critical opinion about the what and why of the story.

The introductory paragraph tells us much about when and under what circumstances, but nothing about who in particular. The grammar of expectation withholds the subjects who will focus our concern. When they do arrive, we already know how dire their plight is, and how ambiguously viewed. And we ought to be more skeptical than the good folk who immortalized Lovell. As I've already suggested, we should note that the relevance of Malvin's analogy (invoking the case of twenty years ago) is undercut by its morally significant differences from the case now at hand. Yet I don't see the discrepancy as evidence of Malvin's bad faith. On the contrary, it seems to be his final gesture in his role as founding father. He—and the community—require a "survivor." Reuben's escape will ensure the posterity and renown which are Malvin's reward. The old man intends to give himself and his "son" the blessing of posterity in the land he has saved. That's "who" Malvin is.

Reuben responds to this vision, but feels guilty for thinking of it at such a moment—as though it were possible to accept the benefit without accepting the sacrifice. What a delusion! Again, seeing more than Reuben does, we should note that Malvin's "generous art" consists of encouraging that delusion. He lets the younger man believe that the penalty for bloodshed can be voided by personal and communal prosperity. Reuben's weakness is due not just to his subconscious desire to live and to marry, but also to his gullibility. He would like to believe in a no-cost victory. And that's "who" *he* is.

And with the death of Malvin, he claims our attention. Things seem to go well for him. He is restored to the settlements. But once he is within that world, he is subject to its view of him. Dorcas and the town are convinced he's a hero. Tales of his valor preempt the truth as gratifyingly as Malvin's analogy took charge in the woods. In neither case does Reuben challenge a story that relieves him of blame. True, he is a coward for not insisting on the truth, but it seems that first Malvin and now the community would prefer not to hear it. Precariously rooted in an alien land, shedding the blood of the native inhabitants, the town has an interest in his being a hero. Believing in him, they think better of themselves, for the honor of his survival means the honor of their own. So once again he appears to escape. But soon it's clear that he hasn't. There is a price for this kind of survival. And now we are "in" to that story. I will not move through it in detail, but will concentrate on the problem of Cyrus, bringing in some concepts from earlier chapters in order to describe the linearity of this story. I shall be looking for more satisfactory answers to the questions surrounding its closure.

In terms of Kronos, or uniformly measured time, Hawthorne's story depicts a grossly arbitrary fate for Cyrus. He is cut off at the very threshold of maturity—as though the year, like his life, were to end on May 12. In terms of Kairos, or humanly significant time, it would seem that Cyrus fares no better. Conceived of as a moral history, his life has contained no sin; in his fifteen years, he has done nothing to deserve the loss of his future. But even as all lives are reenactments of the Fall, every generation is mutually culpable in Adam, and every child is an heir to the drama's last scene. Though Cyrus may be innocent by chronology, he is guilty by typology.

But now let's remember that his life-span fits within the eighteen-year period of Reuben's exile from God. Like Adam, Reuben was presented with alternative plots, alternative futures. Born into the temporal world, he had the chance for an earthly paradise (manifested in domestic bliss, posterity, the "chain of human sympathies") or hell on earth (manifested in a loss of family and community). Malvin's death has meaning for him because he accepts it as the price of America's earthly paradise. Reuben's mistake is in believing that he can inherit that paradise without paying some price. Actually, then, Cyrus' life corresponds not to a Kairos of his own, but to a Kairos of his father's sin-and-blight, a Kairos of life-on-false-premises. In effect, Reuben has remained in his pre-responsible state. He has failed to mature during the eighteen years between the two dates of his presence at the rock. It is as though Cyrus were being denied his existence by virtue of the fact that his father is still a boy.

It is of course the story that has made Cyrus "be"—but not until the last paragraph of the middle section. We are well acquainted with the world of this fiction before Cyrus enters it, and he does so in terms that have already been assigned to his grandfather: he comes created in the terms of frontier adventure and heroism, dressed in the qualities of the hunter and the warrior—the roles in which Malvin had chosen to die, although they more properly belong to his youth than to his maturity as a settled member of the community. Cyrus is created in the terms of— one might almost say by—the hopes and values of the community and of his father: he is a model of the qualities appropriate to the youth of both. Only twice does the language take us within Cyrus' own mind: once when he "[thinks] of the adventurous pleasures of the untrodden forest," and once when he notes the deviation in his father's course and "something began to weigh upon his heart."

Between the happy excitement and the dark premonition comes a long and surprising paragraph. In it we get a vision of an idyllic future, a benign and prosperous life cycle ending in venerable old age for the founder of a dynasty. It is important, I think, that the vision, though apparently an authorial aside, follows directly upon the description of Cyrus' youthful, innocent spirit of adventure—his arrival as an American Adam. It is a reprise of Malvin's prediction for Reuben—but is it now Hawthorne who has resorted to "generous art"? If so, who is being "wiled"? For whose "good"? Hawthorne's evocation of a New England myth comes at a point when the characters may still believe in it. But can we? Not unless we are like the glorifiers of Lovell's Fight. (Or not unless we are like the duped audience of another well-known [and misleading] eulogy of New England's future—the Election Day sermon of the Reverend Arthur Dimmesdale.)

Perhaps the story is about the irresponsibility of traditions, of ameliorated stories that mislead because they promise an Eden without a Fall, a maturity without sacrifice of youth. The strangeness of Reuben's calmness in the face of his son's death, the gross disproportion between the punishment due Reuben and the price paid by Cyrus can, I think, be understood. But it is necessary to see Cyrus as a creature of the frontier's adolescence, living by the terms of a glorified legend. He is doomed by virtue of being these things; he dies "along with," as much as "for" the innocence of a community and the sins of a father. Viewed in this light, Cyrus' death is really not an occasion for rabid anguish, but rather for the saddened acceptance we see.

We, too, can accept it if we have responded to the kind of intensity offered by the prose. In descriptions of Cyrus, words like "youthful" and "adventurous" carry unusual weight, linking him with his grandfather and his father as a young man. Recalling the "spots of *deter-minacy*" discussed in Chapter Two, we might say that Cyrus is an inference we make from these accentuated qualities rather than a character who tends to exhibit them. His death strikes us as the cancellation of these qualities from the world of the story rather than as the removal of a person from life. What a difference it would make if, instead of seeing a model young hunter in pursuit of a deer, we were to know a boy with his own vision of manhood. But the story doesn't offer us that kind of information to assimilate. Cyrus doesn't interfere with our curiosity about Reuben.

The story is a potent example of a home-leaving which turns into a profound homecoming. There is powerful closure, enforced by several typologies: the return to the beginning (defined by geographical place and annual date); the fulfillment of a paradigmatic period of exile from God (see earlier reference to biblical analogues); the completion of a plot sequence of equilibrium (promise to Malvin), disequilibrium (failure to keep it), and new equilibrium (fulfillment in new and more significant terms); the release of energy as the consequences of living by the wrong stories are realized and accepted in the "true" story by Hawthorne. If, in our attempts to reach deferred cognitive closure, we try to rewrite Hawthorne's story, we may simply be supplying our own "memorial of the affair," our own evasions of truth.

"Athénaïse," by Kate Chopin

The Story

Kate Chopin's story is also about unrecognized truth, forces within each character's nature which he or she does not comprehend. In plot, the story is very simple. A young wife runs away from her husband and in the end she comes back. Yet this is one of Chopin's longer stories—twenty-eight ample pages in the Louisiana edition.[15] The eleven numbered sections allow a leisurely, sensuously detailed revelation of a young girl's awakening to womanhood.

Part one finds Cazeau, the girl's husband, eating his dinner alone; she has not yet returned from a visit to her family. He is a stern-faced man, a man who walks over his floors as he rides over his land—wearing spurs. But his voice is gentle and he is wakeful in the springtime night. He must be yearning for his bride. In the second part, Cazeau sets out to bring her home to her duty. His in-laws, he knows, will be little help. The mother of Athénaïse is well-meaning but weak-willed. She indulges her children, helping them postpone their maturity. The younger brother,

15. Chopin, "Athénaïse."

Montéclin, is a wonderful example of Chopin's Creole gallants; he is romantic in a shallow, cocky way. Vaguely jealous of Cazeau's older, firmer, more manly nature—and his control over Athénaïse—Montéclin wants to play hero. So, when his sister says she prefers *not* to return with her husband, Montéclin is happy. He waves his offer of protection. Cazeau hardly notices it. The two men are as different as a *billet doux* and a bill of lading.

Under the inexorable pressure of Cazeau's calm authority, and the inevitability of the institution of marriage itself, Athénaïse grudgingly obeys. But, to emphasize her pique, she rides full speed ahead of her husband on the way back to Cane River. The route takes them through a fallow meadow in the middle of which stands a single large oak tree— "a landmark for ages." Passing the tree, Cazeau has a vivid memory of a childhood experience which occurred on that very same spot. His father had captured a runaway slave and was bringing him home.

> [Cazeau] was a very small boy that day, seated before his father on horseback. They were proceeding slowly, and Black Gabe was moving on before them at a little dog-trot. Black Gabe had run away, and had been discovered back in the Gotrain swamp. They had halted beneath this big oak to enable the negro to take breath; for Cazeau's father was a kind and considerate master, and every one had agreed at the time that Black Gabe was a fool, a great idiot indeed, for wanting to run away from him. (p. 433)

We are told that the adult Cazeau feels "the whole impression was for some reason hideous," but he does not consciously admit to himself the obvious parallel: a husband bringing his wife home against her will is like a master bringing a slave back to his chains. In that case, the "love" of the husband may be as great a mockery as the "kind[ness]" of the master. Anyway, the authority of both is ignoble.

In the third, fourth, and fifth sections we learn more about Athénaïse and the nature of her unhappiness. First of all, we discover that it is not Cazeau personally who offends her, but the state of matrimony itself. She's a romantic young thing, "a chile in character." Under Cazeau's influence she is supposed to grow up, gain maturity. Instead, she's grown fretful. How, where, can she suddenly find the depth and stability needed for the role of a matron? She isn't interested in the business of managing a house. Nor is she emotionally and physically ready for the intimacies of married life. They repel her. And so—willful, restless, truly miserable—she finally gives in to her brother's pettish bravado, his dandified chivalry. With his connivance, she runs away in the night.

Cazeau, hurt and puzzled, warns Montéclin that he will be held responsible for the young girl's safety. But Cazeau refrains from imposing his will. He has come to feel that the marriage was a mistake, but, more importantly, he has come to realize he can't force it to work. His love is constant, deep, and freed now from any unworthy association with power and property. He doesn't want to do anything to bring back the "sensation of baseness" he experienced when passing the oak tree. Never again, therefore, will he compel his wife to return.

The next five parts of the story take place in New Orleans, where Athénaïse is well provided for in a genteel boardinghouse. Montéclin has paid one month's rent. The whole arrangement excites Athénaïse. Here there are no spurs or commands, only flowers and flattery. Sylvie, the landlady, pampers her, and the sunny graciousness of the life melts her anger and bitterness. All that's needed is a channel for other emotions. Conveniently, that is provided by a second boarder, the well-bred man of the world, Gouvernail. He befriends her in her charming ignorance of town life, accepts her willing confidences, and finds himself deeply attracted to her. According to his own code, he feels bound to respect her helplessness, to refrain from sexual advances. Yet he stays near, hoping for the day when the current of her instincts will guide her to his arms. In fact she goes only so far as to cry on his shoulder. What leads her there is an overflow of homesickness, on the crest of which she turns to him for brotherly support; controlling himself, he pretends to be Montéclin. But as the time approaches when she must find her own way in the world, Athénaïse becomes less and less buoyant, confessing that she feels "heart-sick, body-sick." Finally the landlady explains to her that she is pregnant.

The story turns on this revelation, on the fact that it is a total surprise to her. Perhaps the young wife's ignorance is an indictment of her upbringing. But Chopin makes no comment. Instead, she shows how the realization of the pregnancy does, in a matter of minutes, what all of Cazeau's love and duty had failed to accomplish. It makes a woman of her.

> One mood quickly followed another, in this new turmoil of her senses, and the need of action became uppermost. Her mother must know at

once, and her mother must tell Montéclin. And Cazeau must know. As she thought of him, the first purely sensuous tremor of her life swept over her. She half whispered his name, and the sound of it brought red blotches into her cheeks. She spoke it over and over, as if it were some new, sweet sound born out of darkness and confusion, and reaching her for the first time. She was impatient to be with him. Her whole passionate nature was aroused as if by a miracle. (p. 451)

The story now moves swiftly to its close. Athénaïse, asserting her position as Cazeau's wife, uses his credit to make purchases for the baby. We gather that from now on she will be sewing baby clothes, not ball gowns. Having notified Cazeau and arranged for Montéclin to take her home, she parts from Gouvernail in friendly but preoccupied haste. Poor Gouvernail. Frustrated and even aching a bit, he yields her up with gentlemanly grace. At least in this story, he has no further claim on her.

The story ends with Athénaïse returning to her husband's arms. There, for the first time, she meets his kiss with a passion of her own. It is the floodtide of feeling. We have to believe that, in surrendering to Cazeau, she is really claiming her womanhood. Now, at last, she is capable of loving, of caring. As she rises from her husband's embrace, she notices the crying of a child somewhere on the plantation. The last words of the story are these: "'Listen, Cazeau! How Juliette's baby is crying! Pauvre ti chou, I wonder w'at is the matter with it?'" (p. 454).

The Critics

As we have seen, criticism of "Roger Malvin's Burial" has its own biography, which to some extent reflects changing periods in critical fashion. But almost all of the activity seems earnest and sophisticated. By contrast, work on Chopin's stories begins, so to speak, "younger," matures more slowly, may not even yet be "serious," and is hardly effete or contentious. As far as I know, the longest commentary on "Athénaïse" extends to no more than four or five pages, and most of that space is devoted to plot summary.

In early Chopin criticism, the favorite word is "instinctive." According to Leonidas R. Whipple, in 1907, "her technique has the instinctiveness of genius."[16] Daniel S. Rankin, in 1932, is still speaking of her "nat-

16. Whipple, ["Kate Chopin"], 864.

ural story-telling ability and . . . instinctive delicacy." [17] Many of the stories do seem like artless vignettes, the kind that a lady of quick eye, ear, and pen might enclose in a letter. But she can also give the poise of the French *conte* to a humorous tale of the backwoods. Guy de Maupassant is most frequently named as her master, but Flaubert, Gautier, and Daudet are also mentioned. From them she learned "restraint, flexibility, exquisite taste and proportion, finish, and an inevitable *dénouement*." [18] But the apparently well-known fact that Mrs. Chopin wrote impulsively and almost never revised encouraged the view of her as a natural genius almost inadvertently polished by contact with the French masters of the short tale.

Pattee claims that "no writer of the period was more spontaneously and inevitably a story teller. There is an ease and a naturalness about her work that comes from more than mere art." [19] In 1926, Dorothy A. Dondore reemphasized Chopin's sympathy and tolerance—again qualities of nature rather than of art:

> Her main sources of strength are her lack of established prejudices and her interest in the individual. . . . She presents [the Acadians] . . . without the sneers of the early travellers, without the romantic idealization of a Longfellow, but with the sympathy born of her varied ancestry. . . . Perhaps it is her impartiality, her interest in the event rather than the thesis that gives her work its freshness and spontaneity. . . . She attains with a French simplicity of means a French poignancy of effect. Her studies in *Bayou Folk* (1894) are entirely realistic in tone, yet partake of that witchery inherent since the very earliest days in the Southwest's pastoral life. [20]

Rankin sums it all up with a flourish:

> Writing, to Kate Chopin, was spontaneous. Her short stories were published for the most part in their original form. Their shapeliness or semblance of shapeliness was what her mind gave them and her pen put down without revision. Her success as a writer of short stories is a quaint ironic comment on the whole subject of literary modes and the short-story art. In style and design her writing is not art that conceals art. It is spontaneous success. Without any of the tricks of style she achieves the effect of style through simplicity and deftness. [21]

17. Rankin, *Kate Chopin*, 130.
18. Whipple, ["Kate Chopin"], 865.
19. Pattee, *A History of American Literature Since 1870*, 364–65.
20. Dondore, "Kate O'Flaherty Chopin," 90–91.
21. Rankin, *Kate Chopin*, 140.

I should hasten to say that I am not the only one who disagrees with the imputation of artlessness and the derogation of short story "art." But that is not the immediate issue. What is important is that Kate Chopin wrote at a time when literary regionalism was in vogue, when magazines such as *The Century* offered a market for the apparently ingenuous sketch, and when William Dean Howells, for one, felt that women writers had a peculiar knack for the "slight" genre of short fiction. Both the praise and the censure of the early 1900s are more descriptive than analytical—gestures of courtesy or of mockery, the lifted hat or the flicked cigar.

Yet it was not politeness that included her in the 1948 *Literary History of the United States*. It was necessity. Her two collections of short stories, *Bayou Folk* (1894) and *A Night in Acadie* (1897), were well-established volumes of Louisiana fiction. She had to be considered along with George Washington Cable (and ahead of Grace King, Mary Murfree, and Ruth McEnery Stuart) as a local colorist of prime importance to the literature of the South. Along with Sarah Orne Jewett and Willa Cather, she had to be noted as a major woman writer of the late 1800s. The article in the *Literary History of the United States* stresses her development of "virgin territory for fiction," the "Mid-Louisiana parishes of Natchitoches and Avoyelles." There is the usual praise for her "Gallic finesse," her "feeling for character . . . supported by an almost instinctive grasp of form and pace," but there is also a more specific comment on her themes. "Many of [the stories] . . . turn upon acts of rebellion."[22] In *Literature of the American People* (1951), Clarence Gohdes adds that "her emphasis . . . was primarily on character delineation." He goes on to mention her novel, *The Awakening*, calling it an important example of "sterner realism."[23] It seems the writer of charming tales had written a serious novel. Could "instinct" and "spontaneity" explain this phenomenon?

Undoubtedly Chopin criticism comes of age with Kenneth Eble's article "A Forgotten Novel: Kate Chopin's *The Awakening*." At the time he is writing in 1956, he can still say: "Today, Kate (O'Flaherty) Chopin is chiefly remembered as a regional writer whose short stories of the Louisiana Creoles are usually compared with the work of George Wash-

22. Baker, "Delineation of Life and Character," 855, 858, 859.
23. Gohdes, "Exploitation of the Provinces," 654.

ington Cable and Grace King . . . . Her present literary rank is probably somewhere between Octave Thanet (Alice French) and Sarah Orne Jewett."[24] Eble then goes on to establish the value of Chopin's novel, emphasizing its beauty of construction, the coherence and power of its imagery. After the reprinting of *The Awakening*, Chopin's reputation, delicately shaded in before, now is boldly defined. Anyone can see it. She is the American Flaubert, the creator of a genuine masterpiece, a harbinger of American naturalism, and a pioneer in the realistic portrayal of female experience. Modern readers are shocked to realize that, in its own time, the book was regarded as indecent, that the reviewers were impertinent, and that their reaction so depressed Mrs. Chopin that she curtailed her writing. It is a kind of double suicide—the heroine of her novel swims out to sea, and the author drops into silence. Articles and theses line up to defend her.

The mature phase of Chopin criticism begins in the fifties and expands in 1970 with the publication of a *Complete Works* and a critical biography by Per Seyersted. Since her novel is the main focus for most of this work, I won't try to review it but will concentrate now on references to the stories and "Athénaïse" in particular. From the beginning, sympathetic critics have recognized that many of her tales are more than a record of local eccentricities. They deal with universal, and usually elementary, themes, especially the emotion of love, and particularly the psychological intricacies and physical sensations connected with the birth of passion. But how good are they as stories? The question remains open.

At least one critic sees the tales only as sociological indices.[25] Another—Larzar Ziff—puts Chopin in the context of *The American 1890's*, but is also the first to see the end of the story as a function of its aesthetic as much as of the character's fate. For Ziff, Athénaïse is not just a type, nor a study of female psychology, but an individual character, a phase of whose life defines the span and closure of a story.[26]

George Arms pursues the question of Chopin's artistry in "Kate Chopin's *The Awakening* in the Perspective of Her Literary Career" (1967). While acknowledging the importance of the theme of sexual

24. Eble, "A Forgotten Novel," 261–62.
25. Fletcher, "The Southern Woman in the Fiction of Kate Chopin," 128.
26. Ziff, *The American 1890's*, 298–99.

freedom, he argues for a Chopin who is a serious and controlled artist, who can create characters obedient to the laws of their fictional world rather than to the vicissitudes of a locality *or* of an author's life. Arms is interested in Edna Pontellier, the heroine of *The Awakening*, but he speaks of the stories, too, where he finds "contrasts of purpose and aimlessness, of romance and realism, and of sleep and awakening." Confirming Ziff's view of the ending of "Athénaïse," he explains that Chopin "sees truth as constantly reforming itself and as so much a part of the context of what happens that it can never be final or for that matter abstractly stated."[27] Her better stories—and he counts "Athénaïse" as one of the five best in *A Night in Acadie*—develop conflicts that are not resolved at the end, despite the apparent neatness of closure. In short, although he uses a different vocabulary, Arms seems to be arguing that the dynamic of the best stories leads to that "openness" which Robert Adams found to be characteristic of modern fiction. Arms does seem to think the story deserves further notice. He wants to add to its critical stature. But his essay has another mission. It is mainly about Edna. Oddly enough, it appears that the success of *The Awakening*, so long "forgotten," has diverted attention from the stories. People now think of Chopin as a novelist. In 1968, Lewis Leary even derogates the tales, calling them exploitations of "lovable eccentricities." He feels the characters remain sketchy. "Motivation, when present, seems superimposed rather than an inevitable precursor of action."[28] Taken by themselves, these words turn back the clock on Chopin criticism.

But Per Seyersted is one person who has helped to keep interest in the stories alive and growing. As her biographer, he naturally spreads his critical attention more broadly over her work. Regarding "Athénaïse" as one of Chopin's finest achievements, he gives the most detailed commentary on the story that I've yet discovered. Theme is still for him the salient factor: the story is "a deep protest against woman's condition [while not forgetting its sensuous joys]."[29] Echoing her earliest critics, he sees her as "an instinctive teller of stories" (p. 130), but he insists that "she was very conscious of technique, both in matters of detail and of form. Her best tales are fully born, organic entities, firmly controlled,

27. Arms, "Kate Chopin's *The Awakening*," 222.
28. Leary, "Kate Chopin's Other Novel," 60–74.
29. Seyersted, *Kate Chopin*.

and entirely satisfying works of art which show that she knew exactly what she was doing. 'Athénaïse' is a case in point. Here is art concealing art" (p. 130).

After summarizing the story and agreeing with Arms's view of open-mindedness, Seyersted concludes that "the story is governed by a many-sided view of the female condition. Its focus is on woman's role in the life cycle, and this emphasis is subtly supported by the imagery. . . . What makes Cazeau draw a parallel between Athénaïse and a slave is the sight of the oak-tree in the meadow and the smell of elderberry; when she runs away, she inhales the odor of the fields, and just before she learns of her pregnancy, she is homesick for the woods and 'the scent of the ploughed earth'" (p. 132). He goes on to describe the function of the oak tree as the central symbol in the story. In my own discussion, I will refer to many of these same images, but instead of connecting them with the themes of the story, I will deal with them in terms of its reality warp.

Perhaps the most evenhanded statement on Kate Chopin's work comes in 1970, when William M. Gibson, writing for the *Times Literary Supplement*, reviews the LSU Press volumes and the Seyersted biography. In introducing Chopin's work to the English audience, Gibson reminds them of other nineteenth-century writers—like Melville and Dickinson—who achieved proper recognition only in the following century. Chopin, too, is being restored. Gibson narrates her return to prominence. He does find that "her talent is rather less apparent in the short fiction than in her novel. . . . but her best tales demonstrate a vivid sense of the local and temporal . . . and a deep awareness of the truths of the human heart in the vein of Hawthorne and Faulkner." Once again, the story of "Athénaïse" is retold, with Gibson concluding that "in 'Athénaïse,' Chopin gave life again to the old notion that 'the falling out of faithful friends renewing is of love,' with a difference: a considerate love and an unborn child are the means of renewal. But the author's finest touch is surely to permit Cazeau, when he brings his young wife home again, to see himself somehow like his father recapturing Black Gabe, and to vow that his wife will in the future return to him only of her own free will."[30] As will be seen, I, too, feel that the

---

30. Gibson, "Love in Louisiana," 1163.

change in Cazeau is an important part of the story's design. But certainly for the purposes of this chapter Gibson is to be thanked for putting this lady author in the same room with such pipe-smokers as Hawthorne and Faulkner.

She enters the company of two other male giants in the first genre-based study of her tales—the essay on "Kate Chopin's Lyrical Short Stories," by Bert Bender. He begins by prying her away from the local color movement and the Brander Matthews "short-story," and sitting her down with Whitman and Lawrence.

> The lyrical voice embodied in Kate Chopin's short fictions is the antithesis of both the formal rigidity and the genteel, comic tone of the "short-story." Variations on the theme of awakening to ecstatic self-realization, her stories are fictional songs of the self. In them, she affirms aspects of the self that conventions denied, affirms them in a way that resembles Whitman when he sings approvingly of "forbidden voice,/Voices of sexes and lusts." But her stories do not locate, as *Leaves of Grass* does, a mythic self as the synthetic, integrating center of a larger democratic context. The characters depicted in her fictions are tragically set off from their social surroundings, because, like D. H. Lawrence's characters, their awakened identities are at odds with social conventions.[31]

Obviously, "Athénaïse" would be an important story to Bender. And indeed he spends two pages summarizing it, quoting at length from the oak-tree and realization-of-pregnancy scenes. But his final words are about the familiar thematic issues, about the "awakening of an ecstatic knowledge and acceptance of her biological destiny" (p. 264). Like other students of lyricism in the short story (see Chapter One), Bender does not escape the tautological emphasis on song, impulse, unconventional feeling, and organic imagery. Nevertheless, his article is an important first step in the direction of serious, genre-based criticism of the story.

I would like to take the next step right here. To do so, I will not have to argue that Chopin is a better short story writer than she is a novelist; as a matter of fact, I agree that *The Awakening* is her major work in every sense. Nor will I have to sort out a variety of interpretations, as in the case of "Roger Malvin's Burial." In "Athénaïse," the point has always seemed obvious enough; instead, there have been implied dis-

31.   Bender, Bert, "Kate Chopin's Lyrical Short Stories," 259.

agreements over literary method, merit, and consequence. But I do not even want to end the debate over whether she does or does not use "art to conceal art." I'd rather consider whether her "instinct" might not lead us to certain intrinsic qualities of short fiction, and whether her "calculation" might not point to certain formal properties of the genre. By approaching the story in the manner used throughout this book, I hope to describe it in a way more helpful to the student of short story aesthetics.

Hymen and Eros

The first word of "Athénaïse" is—"Athénaïse." Here is the first paragraph:

> Athénaïse went away in the morning to make a visit to her parents, ten miles back on rigolet de Bon Dieu. She did not return in the evening, and Cazeau, her husband, fretted not a little. He did not worry much about Athénaïse, who, he suspected, was resting only too content in the bosom of her family; his chief solicitude was manifestly for the pony she had ridden. He felt sure those "lazy pigs," her brothers, were capable of neglecting it seriously. This misgiving Cazeau communicated to his servant, old Félicité, who waited upon him at supper. (p. 426)

Although the wife's name is the opening word, and although the verb sends her off on a journey, the reader is left behind with the husband. Athénaïse "went away"—the diction is almost childlike, and certainly the intensity is low at this point—but it takes us only four prepositional phrases to learn what we'd know if we were living in Cazeau's world: when ("in the morning"), why ("to make a visit"), and where ("ten miles back on the rigolet de Bon Dieu"). The information is mostly for our benefit, to get us very quickly over the ontological gap between our world and the story's—but it is very circumstantial. Very inconclusive.

And now it seems that we get a series of unexpected reversals, denials, replacements. First of all, the beginning of the second sentence withholds the natural complement of the first sentence. The simplest closure, our natural guess, would be: "And she returned in the evening [to resume her life with her husband in his home on Cane River]." In fact what we get is: "She did not return in the evening. . . ." We're left with the direction of "away," the temporariness of "visit," and the syntactic and lexical need for "return." What is preventing this closure? At the moment, only the semantic gap between "here" and "ten miles back," between "her parents" and "her husband." How long can the separation be maintained? How great is the disequilibrium? The answer is the length and the shape of the story.

As we have in the past, let's look at the way syntax and semantics distribute intensity. I mentioned before that "went away" seems very neutral, certainly by comparison with other verbs like "ran away" or "sneaked away." And there seems to be something even more deliberately low-keyed about "fretted not a little." About his wife? Apparently not—but the stated object of his worry lies on the other side of a semicolon. Before we get there we encounter a long relative clause; within it we find the wryness of "suspected," which seems to put bitterness into "only too content," and maybe even sours the sentiment of "in the bosom of her family." Finally we do learn that his worry is for the pony his wife was riding. The family which opens its bosom to Athénaïse is "capable of seriously neglecting" the animal. It does seem strange that the words of apparently deepest and most genuine feeling are reserved for the pony, while there seems to be a grudging tone in the comments on the wife. The valences call attention to themselves, and so we register both the semantically high intensity of words like "seriously" and "chief" *and* the contextually high intensity of the flat or hackneyed diction. In the prose of this story, in its reality warp, the density and intensity are clues to what is *not* on the page.

We've seen the pony moved into the place where we'd expect Athénaïse as the object of her husband's concern. But we've also seen the Miché family moved into the role of the girl's protector. They've replaced Cazeau, and his fear that they will mistreat his pony is at least in part an expression of his own hurt feelings. The energy of his resentment comes through in his heightened concern for the pony and in his contempt for "those lazy pigs, her brothers." It's also likely that, by confiding (up to a point) in his servant, he makes her loyal presence a reproach to his wife. At any rate, there is a sense in which the story can be read only by seeing through the disguise of the text. It's not hard to do. The rules are those of the simplest psychology.

Reading further, we could say that the grammar of expectation keeps us wondering when Athénaïse will come back. Surely the absence of the wife calls loudly for her presence. Yet the story which most critics have felt to be about her frustration has up to now told us only of his. We come to believe in his love despite apparent denials: the show of not caring, maintained for pride's sake; the jangling spur which he wears indoors and which is so patent a symbol of his masculine invasion of the woman's domain; the managerial busyness of his evening work. But now look—the deepening dusk, muted sounds of crying and singing, and later the moonlight, and the "touch of the cool breath of the spring night," the "distant, tireless, plaintive notes of the accordion"—all these images crowd into the world of the story. What are they doing there?

Ostensibly, the last paragraphs of part one are about the failure of a marriage. But again, what Cazeau puts into words, even within his own thoughts, is not all that the prose has to say. It is not, as the words declare, the "unpleasant reflections" on his marriage that hold him awake, but the "touch" of the air and its sounds. "The craving of his whole body" is not, as the proposition states, "for rest and sleep"; it is for Athénaïse. We have been taught to make these substitutions by the adjustments we have had to make to enter the world of this story.

Considering the way we are drawn in, it seems to me more important to establish what we know of the story's world than to paraphrase its themes. As we have in the past, let's begin by examining what gives the story its linear dimension. Several answers are possible, but surely one of the most obvious is this: the stages of maturation from girlhood to wife-and-motherhood (defined as the awakening of the maternal and, concomitantly, the sexual instincts). I would argue that there is also a second and complementary maturation in Cazeau. Let me sketch out both sequences with some further commentary along the way. For Athénaïse,

X_1 = a physical retreat to the rigolet de Bon Dieu.

It would seem as though the wife is trying to regain the status of daughter and sister, to go back several months in time by going "ten miles back" in the bayous. What she does not like are the physical changes of marriage—the dislocation from girlhood, from a life without serious commitments. In her home the mother and younger son are weak-willed and foolish, and the father and older son, though capable of respecting the solid virtues of Cazeau, are nevertheless only renters on the land. Cazeau is an owner. Athénaïse is moving back, temporarily and geographically, to the more casual bonds of life as a Miché.

X_2 = a psychological retreat into a sense of injury.

When she has been brought back against her will, Athénaïse seeks comfort in tears and seclusion. She refuses to take Cazeau's hand offered in token of his willingness to make the best of things, and she rejects her role as mistress of the house by flinging away her bunch of keys. Finally, thinking "that Montéclin was the only friend left to her in the world," she confides her misery to him and accedes to his plan for escape.

X_3 = the physical escape to New Orleans.

Despite the provisions made by Montéclin, and despite the fact that she had been to the city in previous years, Athénaïse is for the first time on her own. True, she is not yet financially independent, but she has gallant—and quite naïve—hopes of finding a job. Her change in locale brings with it a drastic change in her manner of life, most especially freeing her from the supervision of those who have hitherto been responsible for her. On a minor scale, but on a daily basis, she is free to decide what to do.

X_4 = adoption of Gouvernail as friend, brother surrogate, and potential lover.

This change is not really a "retreat." Athénaïse initiates the relationship with Gouvernail by asking him to address and post a letter to her brother—thus making him an innocent accomplice in her adventure. Soon she is pouring out her troubles to his surprised but sympathetic ear. He reciprocates by lending her a magazine to read, and their friendship quickly develops. It serves to introduce Athénaïse to a life of respectable but otherwise unavailable pleasures—visits to the lake, strolls through the French Quarter, little dinners in charming restaurants. It seems that the progression of events might very well lead to an X_5 which should be the acceptance of Gouvernail as a lover.

But all along there has been an undocumented series of X's, namely the physiological consequences of her marriage. These have been hinted at, but only in terms of the offensive intrusion of her husband into her life, her privacy, and, of course, her body. Suddenly the results come to the surface of the story as they come into the consciousness of the heroine:

X_5 = the discovery that she is with child by Cazeau.

Almost everyone writing about this story has quoted the passage in which this "turning point" occurs. Knowledge of her pregnancy does, of course, reverse the direction of Athénaïse's movements in the story, both the retreat from marriage and the attraction to Gouvernail. But we can see that the *peripeteia* is only an illusion created by her delayed awareness. We have seen her resent her husband's ability to carry on his work in the face of her life-shattering troubles—a telling sign that she wants him to care. We have also learned that Gouvernail, an expert on women, suspects she is really in love with her husband. And certainly, as many have noted, the lush imagery of springtime sounds and smells creates the context for a sensual awakening, for the breeding of life.

Personal and social factors have caused the readiness for adult sexuality (Eros) to be out of phase with the timing of the legal marriage (Hymen). The natural cycles of the year and of the womb are the true arbiters of maturity; when they so determine, the woman is born. In other words, the "knowledge" that Sylvie imparts does not educate the girl in any conceptual sense. It merely identifies the biological truth which must eventually dawn on her. And now we remember what everyone—except Cazeau—seems to have known from the start: "People often said that Athénaïse would know her own mind some day. . . . If she ever came to such knowledge, it would be by no intellectual research, by no subtle analyses or tracing the motives of actions to their source. It would come to her as the song to the bird, the perfume and color to the flower" (p. 433). Those who think Chopin does not understand motivation may not understand the implications of these words. Everywhere the imagery reinforces the linear process of natural organic maturation as a force stronger than logical reasoning, stronger than "motive." One "learns" the qualities of being a woman by growing into womanhood.

X_6 = the assumption of the roles of wife and mother.

As several critics have pointed out, the closure here is definitive and satisfying within the terms of the story world. Very literally, this is a home-coming story. Athénaïse returns to the husband she left, and the distant cry of the Negro baby, heard in the first section of the story, is there again at the end; it triggers the final, symbolic gesture of maternal concern.

But what of Cazeau? I mentioned earlier that he, too, experiences a growth of awareness. We might look at the stages of his maturation as a secondary but essential part of the structure. For Cazeau,

Y_1 = denial of deepest feelings.

As a temporarily deserted husband, Cazeau "fretted not a little" in that first paragraph. We've seen that he does not admit his real feelings but hides them behind concern—quite genuine in itself—for the pony. He maintains an air of business as usual. It is this very capacity for self-discipline which aggravates Athénaïse's resentment. But we see beyond it to the feeling it guards, to the yearning which Cazeau does not even admit to himself.

Y_2 = forces Athénaïse to return to his home.

Cazeau finds Athénaïse's continued absence an annoyance. Retrieving her will be an inconvenience in his busy workday, but he sees it as "the task of bringing his wife back to a sense of her duty." When he confronts her in her parents' home and receives her look of reproach, he is "maddened and wounded. . . . But whatever he might feel, Cazeau [knows] only one way to act toward a woman" (p. 431). That "way" is with gentleness and courtesy but with a firmness that allows for no question of his right to give orders. Cazeau's range of responsiveness here is clearly limited. He knows "only one way to act" toward all those in the category of "women." This class noun identifies a category that is not only biologically but socially conditioned for obedience. General-izations about women are so engrained that they preempt any special consideration of the narrower categories, "inexperienced girls" and "Athénaïse." Cazeau has no equipment for dealing with the confused emotions of this particular woman. Neither can he allow his own partic-ular feelings to interfere with what he conceives to be his duty as the man in charge—of his workers, his lands, his livestock, his wife.

Y_3 = gives up "story-book" notions of happiness.

Chopin's fairness, her balanced view of the battle of the sexes, is evident in Cazeau's own confessed illusions. He admits, with dignified candor, that "I expected—I was even that big a fool—I believed that yo' coming yere to me would be like the sun shining out of the clouds, an' that our days would be like w'at the story-books promise after the wedding. I was mistaken" (p. 435). From a less honorable man, these words would seem like recrimination. From someone whose dignity was only swagger, they might be simply ridiculous. But from Cazeau, the admission is both manly and pertinent. Men as well as women are vulnerable to romantic yearnings that have nothing to do with mundane existence or—more importantly—with genuine passion. But we see here that Cazeau can adapt to new perceptions, can correct his presumptions. He, in his own way, can change.

Y_4 = experiences a "humiliating sensation of baseness" when passing the old oak tree.

Cazeau, too, has his burgeoning of consciousness. And, like the awakening of Athénaïse, it is triggered by a heightening of the senses rather than by a sharpening of the mind. Crossing "the old fallow meadow that was level and hard," *i.e.*, yielding no crop, Cazeau sees the tree "that had been a landmark for ages—or was it the odor of elderberry stealing up from the gully to the south? or what was it that brought vividly back to Cazeau, by some association of ideas, a scene of many years ago?" (p. 433). This may be Lockean psychology, the progress from sensation to idea, but here the "idea" remains an image, or rather a series of images which add up to a "whole impression." That impression is "hideous," but the reason for its ugliness is never specified, never rationally perceived. Later, Cazeau refrains from pursuing Athénaïse to New Orleans. Consciously he sees the matter as an issue of pride: "For no woman on earth would he again undergo the humiliating sensation of baseness that had overtaken him in passing the old oak-tree in the fallow meadow" (p. 438). But Chopin has again, as in the opening paragraph, made the prose cut two ways. That class noun "woman" has been intensified to "no woman on earth." He is now judging by life on earth, not in "story-books." The verbs, too, are telling. Pages ago, when first passing the oak tree, Cazeau "spurred his horse to a swift gallop[, o]vertaking his wife." Now we learn that he is the one who was "overtaken."

He is now also the subject of "undergo," a verb that is grammatically transitive but semantically passive. Did we think it was only Athénaïse who is undergoing duress? Cazeau, too, has been acted upon by something beyond his control.

Prompted by his new feeling, Cazeau writes Athénaïse the letter "in which he disclaimed any further intention of forcing his commands upon her." It may seem a rather stiff communication, but its tone and premises are different from those of his previous dealings with Athénaïse. The letter is addressed from one person to another, rather than from a Husband to a Wife. Cazeau is recognizing the woman he loves as someone with a will of her own, with the power to make a choice, and with the right to be a voluntary and reciprocal partner in the union of marriage. It is a letter he could not have written prior to Y_4, and it brings closure to his part of the story.

The pattern of X's, the dominant linearity of Athénaïse's change, shows a progression from retreat to assertion; the pattern of Y's, the secondary linearity of her husband's change, shows a progression from assertion to abeyance. Taken together, they give the story a complexity and balance that most thematic readings have missed. The *Kairos* of the story, the humanly significant span of time it covers, is clearly a period of maturation. But it includes not only the woman's but the man's awakening.

Viewed holistically, as a spatial design, the story is a pair of converging "biorhythms"—as they'd be called today. Gouvernail, remember, introduces the idea that marriage, as an institution, is irrelevant. What properly arranges sexual union is the mutual desire of the people involved, whether married or not. It may have been a liberal view in the 1890s, it may have been "daring" as an opinion, but as a description of the forces at work in the world, it seems only a faithful account. Since the fifties, critics have made this argument their theme. Although there has been praise for the control of imagery, the psychological realism, and the dramatic finesse of the story, that admiration fails to do justice to Chopin's appreciation of short story aesthetics. Many of her tales *are* no more than sketches or vignettes, but in "Athénaïse" she exploits the dual dimensions of linearity and spatiality, the unified *Kairos*, the emblematic sentences, and the powerful closure which help make the peculiar "resistance"—and thus the rhythm—of the short story.

Hawthorne and Chopin

Nothing I could say would increase or diminish the importance of "Roger Malvin's Burial" to historians of American literature. My purpose has been to emphasize the interest of the story to those specifically concerned with short story criticism, and to show that an approach based on an aesthetics of the form can help to sort out if not to resolve contradictions arising among other critics using other approaches. In the case of "Athénaïse," I do indeed hope that I may advance the reputation of a story and an author. Chopin's place as a novelist now seems secure, but as a result, her stories have become places where one looks for hints of the themes and techniques so brilliantly displayed in the long work. "Athénaïse" is from the same period as *The Awakening*. It is a mature piece of work in its own right, and it has certain qualities of special importance: the *Kairos* based mainly on organic cycles, the repetitions within its linear scheme, and the syntactic and semantic maneuvers which force us to replace overt propositions with subliminal semantic content. These qualities make the story an early example of what Baldeshwiler would call the "lyric" short story. Chopin predates Anderson by a generation or more, and might very well be used to initiate studies of the lyrical story in America.

Of even more general interest is the fact that Hawthorne and Chopin seem to resonate when brought together as short story artists. A strange pair, the Salem sage and the Creole muse. Both are open to the mysteries of "the heart," the pull of nature against the curb of law in a "free" land. Such tensions may be thought of as peculiarly American, even peculiarly nineteenth-century American. But the terms I've been using in this chapter are tailored to the genre, not to the period or to the theme. Of course, it has been argued that the genre itself is peculiarly American. Whether or not that's true, I would say that both Hawthorne and Chopin belong to the "classic" tradition of the American short story. In "Roger Malvin's Burial" and "Athénaïse," the story rhythm is defined by a counterpoint of individual variance from the "meter" of society. The expected patterns of a man-made *Kronos*—of public, provincial history in the one case and of institutionalized female destiny in the other—clash with an organic *Kairos* of individual moral or biological maturity. That, I would say, is the essence of the classic American short story.

CHAPTER SEVEN

The Contemporaries

• • •

Probably every teacher and professor of English has taught a short story—once. But stories, as a rule, turn up in the curricula for beginners and "nonmajors," and hardly anyone who teaches graduate students teaches stories—*as such*. Still, flipping through the literary journals, you can always find a study of "The Dead." No doubt the writers of these articles are seriously interested in their work, though they are not so likely to think of themselves as critics of "the short story." Not as Ian Watt is a critic of "the novel." Even those who have written book-length histories of the form (like F. L. Pattee's *The Development of the American Short Story*) seem to feel they have to call attention to the form. They have to put it on the map where others can find it. Yet is there anybody who hasn't been to the House of Usher?

As the result of undergraduate survey courses, there are many people who can tell you how the form developed; how it emerged from the sleepy hollows of Washington Irving, took on the moral and arabesque shapes of Hawthorne and Poe; how it stretched socially and regionally to James and Jewett; how it spoke the vernacular in Calaveras County, turned naturalistic in an open boat, reached deep into the psyche in Winesburg, in Babylon, and, of course, In Our Time; how it branched out southern and suburban and ethnic and far. But most of all how it avoided the sterile formula, the tricky surprise, and the salable sentiment. Furthermore, everyone knows about Poe's "single effect," and many even know about Welty's "place." But does anybody know where the story is now?

In organizing fiction for discussion, it seems a chronology is less appropriate than a spectrum; thus, I'd put the "experimental" story across from, not after, the "traditional" one. Stories of all kinds are being written now. Indeed, they offer a convenient point of entry for those who are curious about contemporary fiction. But I've been arguing all along that we need to see short fiction as generically different from long fiction. And if these ideas have more than a quaint appeal, they should be of some use in discriminating among the colors on the spectrum of stories. They should enable us not only to compare and contrast individual works but to recognize and experience the uniqueness of each. So I would like to discuss in detail three stories by authors very different from each other. The stories have been chosen because they are relatively short, recent, well executed, theoretically significant, and roughly comparable in subject. In each, a woman's self-control is seriously threatened.

"Order of Insects," by William H. Gass

In his preface to the 1976 edition of *In the Heart of the Heart of the Country*, Gass tells us that "the contemporary American writer is in no way a part of the social and political scene."[1] He reminds us that we rarely copy the dress and hairstyles of our prominent writers, that we do not elect them to office or seek their help in a crisis. They are themselves, we guess, in a continual state of upset, of malaise and frustration, and while we might suspect that their chronic alienation is the result of their being treated as wards of academia, or as talk-show dolls and publishers' pets, it is just as easy to think they deserve nothing better. Like Rip Van Winkle, they love ale and gossip, hate plows and accounts. All they have to offer is a tale. Now if art is critique, and if we dearly need such criticism, then we should take very seriously the wagging of a tale. But what if the wag is only chasing his tail?

Gass explains that he became a writer in order to turn himself from a nonentity, mired in midwestern inconsequence, into a rhythm of beautiful sounds, a voice that mattered—to himself, primarily, but also to others. Meaning, worth, justification—all reside in the construct of the language itself. But do not end there. A fiction, says Gass, is a "figure of

1. Gass, Preface . . . , 12.

life." Totally coherent, verbally sufficient, it is a large-scale metaphor for something in our lives. It is also, in the particular case of fictions by Gass, the figure of a law—epistemological, ontological—of life. Here is the first sentence of "Order of Insects."

> We certainly had no complaints about the house after all we had been through in the other place, but we hadn't lived there very long before I began to notice every morning the bodies of a large black bug spotted about the downstairs carpet; haphazardly, as earth worms must die on the street after a rain; looking when I first saw them like rolls of dark wool or pieces of mud from the children's shoes, or sometimes, if the drapes were pulled, so like ink stains or deep burns they terrified me, for I had been intimidated by that thick rug very early and the first week had walked over it wishing my bare feet would swallow my shoes.[2]

One hundred and nineteen words that suck you right into story. The ontological gap seems rather slight at first. There's a lambent dailiness about the first clause—who hasn't heard somebody say "we had no complaints . . . after all we had been through." Yet, colloquially, it would've been "we'd." All we'd been through. That "we," though, is familiar: the domestic pronoun of the householding couple. "But we hadn't lived there very long before I began to notice every morning. . . ." Indeterminate past yields to specified time; married "we" turns to single "I"; generalized "living" is now a "noticing."

Every morning I notice—what? "The bodies of a large black bug spotted about the downstairs carpet." A student of mine, reading this story with firm inquisitiveness, pointed out to me that Gass was ungrammatical. After all, how many bodies can a single bug have? "The bodies of a large black bug." "Well," I said, "this 'bug' is generic. Don't we say 'the nations of man?'" "Yes," she said, "but we don't say the nations of a man." "Ah, but say we're anthropologists," I backed, trying hard to fill. "And we discover a burial ground with the skeletons of twenty warriors. After much study, we announce: 'These are the bones of a large white man.'" These are the bodies of a large black bug. And when those words enter our minds, we are adjusted ever so subtly into science. We are going to learn about an order of bugs—and we'd better be curious.

2. Gass, "Order of Insects," 163.

A series of comparisons follow: the bodies are like 1) worms dead on the street after a rain, 2) rolls of dark wool, 3) pieces of mud from children's shoes, 4) ink stains, and 5) burns. The domain of the imagery is domestic, familiar. These are all examples of untidyness, out-of-placeness: worms out of the garden and onto the pavement, mud out of the yard and into the livingroom, ink off the desk and onto the floor, ashes out of the pipe and onto the rug. All are the normal disarrangements that make housekeeping necessary. They are dis-orders from the point of view of "the wife of the house."

And this lady is sensitive. She fears to mar the perfection of the rug by walking over it in shoes. She is "intimidated." Now, if she were the sort who couldn't bear to use plates for fear of sliming their shine, we would suspect our lady of "problems." But as it is, she is not so unlike most of us, who would hesitate before staining an ivory plush. We can understand the reluctance, the shrinking, the wish that it could be our stocking feet, not our streetwise shoes, that touched the new dress of the floor. We might have wished that our shoes would swallow our feet. For shoes can do that, in a simple metaphorical act—one that violates the inanimate feature of shoes, while preserving the logic of shoes vis-à-vis feet. But what does it take to express the reluctance as she does? To want our feet to swallow our shoes? That's something else again.

That is a complex rearrangement of semantics. For shoes have, normally, the features of toughness and hollowness. Feet are relatively tender and solid. Shells, too, are tough and hollow; like shoes, they are an outer protection. Bodies, like feet, are tender and solid; they live inside shells. The foot inside the shoe is like the body inside the shell. Now there is an order of beings, including roaches, that are exoskeletal, having their bony structure on the outside, as a shell; there is another order, including humans, which are endoskeletal, having their bony structure on the inside. Thus, the shoe-covered foot is imitating the exoskeletal form of the roach. By swallowing its shoe, the foot internalizes its shell and is human again. Is this our lady's image—or our author's little game?

At this point it is worth noting that we have traveled through considerable density, have in fact negotiated a sentence with two sets of compound main clauses, several subordinate clauses, and a handful of assorted modifiers. The interference to closure is perceptible; we must absorb all that I have hitherto been discussing—and more—before the period is reached. As for intensity, it is present in a way that is characteristic of Gass, and of this story. The elaborate dailiness and ordinariness of the diction is felt, I think, as deliberate—especially given the actual formality of the syntax. These are common words, but no common speech. This is a highly "written" sentence, as we come to appreciate more and more as we note the semantic play discussed above. "Bug" is not necessarily a high-intensity word, though it carries connotations of disgust. Ordinarily "swallow" would not catch our attention, but here it is forced to act strangely. On the other hand, "downstairs carpet" and "drapes" retain much of their customary neutrality, while "terrified" and "intimidated" carry a definite (though perhaps less strong than usual) charge. Knowing what we do of Gass's theory of fiction, we should expect just what we find: a dense prose with highly arbitrary conditioning of intensity.

It is hard, too, not to let the word "roach" awaken memories of literary antecedents. Probably the most famous "bug" story ever written is Kafka's "Metamorphosis." There a man wakes to find he has become, quite literally, a cockroach. In Gass's story, a woman's consciousness awakens to the precise and beautiful lawfulness in the structure and movements of the cockroach. She will arrive at an appreciation that reverses—rather than emblematically points to—the norms of ordinary life. This woman will achieve a kind of thinking that operates on reality the way topological mathematics operates on the doughnut to show its equivalence to the coffee cup. We will observe her gradually achieving this philosophical view. And where we have a process, we may look for linearity.

Each sentence after the first one adds fragments of observed data. If there is an insistent linearity in this story, it is probably in the sequence of her detailed "reactions." In other words, there is a series we might identify as X_1 through X_n. After the initial description of her wonder, she gets down to giving us a narrative.

> X_1: "At first I reacted as I should, bending over wondering what in the world; yet even before I recognized them I'd withdrawn my hand, shuddering." (p. 164)

Normal, feminine, automatic, this reaction is mindless. It is associated with memories of nightmarish horrors, for she now recalls "the red ants in our kitchen," which, as one might expect, her husband disposed of. This response is on the level of primitive instinct reinforced by domestic role playing.

As she goes on to tell us "I never think of their species as alive," we realize that something intervenes in the series of X's. The narrative voice is brooding, meditating, filling in commentary from a point of view above the level of narrative chronology. So we will see the effect of some X's before we encounter them in the narrative. For example we learn quite soon now that at some point she developed a scientific curiosity about her bugs. She has reached the level of technical definition. Consulting her French handbook of insects, she finds out that these bugs are a common, vulgar nuisance. "Nevertheless they are a new experience" for her. Furthermore, the French text of the handbook, by translating the ordinary English into a more "elegant tongue," reinforces and parallels the translation of usually repugnant experience into an appreciation of beauty. Typically, for Gass, understanding comes through a heightened sensitivity to language. Empirically, our lady has observed two kinds of roach bodies; when she learns the technical names for them, "adult" and "nymph," she is struck by the strange burdens and strange travels of words: "Nymph. My god the names we use." But she can say, with perfect authority, that "the nymph was a rich golden color deepening in its interstices to mahogany." And she can tell us what each one looked like "under a glass." Clearly, then, there has been an important change in the way she looks at these bugs:

X_2: "I've a collection now I keep in typewriter-ribbon tins. . . ."
(p. 166)

She has become a collector, a scientific examiner, a student. Her observations lead her quite naturally to another speculation: "I suspect if we were as familiar with our bones as with our skin, we'd never bury dead but shrine them in our rooms." She has learned that "corruption in these bugs is splendid." It is another semantic conversion, brought about by deep penetration into the particular: in these bugs, corruption is ugly and splendid—all instincts and casual assumptions to the contrary. So great is the turnaround, that it extends to a change in her life.

X_3: ". . . the whole change, the recent alteration in my life, was the consequence of finally coming near to something." (p. 167)

Initially (and we now have a reference back to X_1 and X_2), "it was a self-mortifying act." She'd felt horror, nausea, but also "the worst of angers." Rapidly, she now breaks down the X_2 into the steps of her observation, gives us the bits of information that collected as she came back again and again for a closer look. The result? Yet a more drastic change in her life:

X_4: "I no longer own my own imagination." (p. 167)

She becomes obsessed with the idea of the bug, going now beyond the limits of empirical observation. As she lies in bed, she dreams of them materializing on the carpet. Ultimately, her imagination allows her to alter the way she perceives her own body: "I lay shell-like in our bed, turned inside out." Under these constraints of this new law of being, she can see the roach's beautiful carcass as its soul, which "was the same as the dark soul of the world itself." She adds, "It was this beautiful and terrifying feeling that took possession of me finally." The incidence of high-intensity words ("beautiful," "terrifying") might be expected here, as the philosophical appreciation of order leads her through the veil of appearances to the calculus of being. This is the eerie ecstasy of a Ptolemy, an Einstein. After this climax she loops back, through another self-analysis, to "resee" the X_1: "the first [bugs] I came on looked put together in Japan" and "so it was amid the worries of our ordinary life I bent, innocent and improperly armed, over the bug that had come undone. Let me think back on the shock. . . ."

By now she can see that initial shock as an ontological one. She can compare it to other ordinary shocks—a burn, the news of someone's death, the fear of illness within her own body. This new shock was, she perceives, of another order entirely. Coming closer to herself, she can see with a more fierce precision. "I said I was innocent. Well I was not. Innocent. My god the names we use." The verbatim echo is the knell of illusion. "The eye never ceases to change." And what the eye of this woman sees now is "the dark soul of the world."

X_5: "my terror has another object . . . I feel as though I'd been entrusted with a kind of eastern mystery, sacred to a dreadful god, and I am full of the sense of my unworthiness and the clay of my vessel." (p. 169)

Holding the bug in her hand, she knows that "there is a fierce joy in its composition that beggars every other." Already she has transcended the empirical terrors of life; now she has transcended its ordinary joys.

Such perception is surprising in a woman, she says. And so she "[takes] up their study with a manly passion." She notes that "caterpillars are a simple section of intestine . . . yet when they crawl their curves conform to graceful laws." She is like Galileo, who "found in the pendulum its fixed intent." But there is a limit to the human eye's power to gaze on abstract law. Having assumed the eyes of the scientist, the philosopher, and the mystic, there is really only one more transformation left:

X_6: "This point of view I tremble in is the point of view of a god, and I feel certain, somehow, that could I give myself entirely to it, were I not continuing a woman, I could disarm my life, find peace and order everywhere." (p. 171)

Knowing her husband can offer only husbandly help, she dreams again of abandoning her shell, of being free to gambol in harmony with the music of the spheres. But the pull of human gravity brings her back. Here is the last sentence of the story:

How can I think of such ludicrous things—beauty and peace, the dark soul of the world—for I am the wife of the house, concerned for the rug, tidy and punctual, surrounded by blocks. (p. 171)

Here, then, we have the final reaction. But which of the following is it?

X_n: I realized my temporary insanity.
X_n: I am housebound (and all that that implies) forever.
X_n: I've experienced a glimpse into the world of pure law and will never be the same again.

Our choice may depend on our perception of the story's spatiality.

Most obviously, the overall design is achieved through the looped returns to the act of examining, in detail, a particular something brought close. In his preface, the author tells us how fundamental this activity is:

Nature rarely loops. Nature repeats. This spring is not a former spring rethought, but merely another one, somewhat the same, somewhat not. However, in a fiction, ideas, perceptions, feelings, return like reconsiderations, and the more one sees a piece of imaginative prose as an adventure of the mind, the more the linearities of life will be bent and interrupted.

That is why, by the way, a concept of linearity in fiction based on chronology is inappropriate. But watch how Gass explains himself:

> Just as the revision itself is made of meditative returns, so the reappearance of any theme constitutes the reseeing of that theme by itself. Otherwise there is no advance. There is stagnation. The quiet spiral of the shell, a gyre, even a whirlwind, a tunnel towering in the air: these are the appropriate forms, the rightful shapes; yet the reader must not succumb to the temptations of simple location, but experience in the rising, turning line the wider view, like a sailplane circling through a thermal, and sense at the same time a corkscrewing descent into the subject, a progressive deepening around the reading eye, a penetration of the particular.[3]

Or, as he puts it earlier, "an exploration of an image." The story follows the spiraling movement of the narrator's mind centered on her study of the bug but swinging in ever more ambitious arcs through richer realms of implication. Our series of seven X's identifies these levels as: the instinctual, the scientific, the moral, the imaginative, the mystical, the godlike, and the human. This is a sequence—both hierarchic and cyclic —that is fundamental to Western philosophy. Its law defines not the music of spheres but the orbit of thought. In its beautiful attunement to that law, the story, about a simple section of experience, has its curves, and they, too, "conform to graceful laws."

As we move through the series of X's, and as we come to an appreciation of the law they follow, we gradually assimilate what we need to achieve closure. Periodicity is felt in the emphasis of dailiness, but also in the subtle shift from the "morning" act of "notice" to the nighttime speculation. We pass through many calendar days but only one day's cycle. In the sense of rhythm as resistance overcome, we may say that we are brought to that equilibrium of impasse: we've shared the transcendent insight; we see again its human limitations. There we are. There she is. There are a great many of Western art's fictional characters, who hang in the ontological balance between a god and a clod.

3. Gass, Preface . . . , 26, 26–27.

"Order of Insects" is a moving story, I think—not least because it is a classic home-leaving story. Our lady has not only taken a new house quite literally, but has left the old hominess of her housewifely fears, in order to enter the world of the gods. She's abandoned the shell of reality as she had narrowly conceived of it. But neither can she enter this heady atmosphere except in dreams, by snatches, and at a cost to her life as a woman. The story itself, as a unit of narrative discourse, is a beautiful, artful integration of repetitive fears and sequential insight.

"First Views of the Enemy," by Joyce Carol Oates

Just around the turn, the road was alive.[4]

Just around the turn of your life, this story begins. Though there are none of the obvious "nonsequential sequence signals," there's the illusion that a road must lead up to this turn as well as around it. We don't yet know what map it's on, what country it crosses, but the existence of country, of movement through it, is predicated as surely as the fact that the road will soon turn. But is it a "fact" that the road is "alive"? We're in the presence of metaphor, and may react to the "literary/aesthetic test" for fictionality. The road is alive in the sense that it is full of beings who are intensely alive, as we might say a decayed log is alive with ants. The next sentence really follows from the first, as though the period were a colon:

> First to assault the eye was a profusion of heads, black-haired, bobbing, and a number of straw hats that looked oddly professional—like straw hats in a documentary film; and shirts and overalls and dresses, red, yellow, beflowered, dotted, striped, some bleached by the sun, some stiff and brilliant, just bought and worn proudly out of the store. (p. 89)

There are people here—somewhere. But they aren't mentioned. Only heads, hats, shirts, overalls, dresses. Yet the next sentence contains a "they" obviously referring back to the unspecified wearers of this flamboyant attire—which looks so "oddly professional," as if worn by the habitual subjects of documentary films. "They" are Mexican peasants, hungry, vital migrant workers on the road to jobs in North America. Their bus has broken down. Enter, upon the scene, an American

---

4. Oates, "First Views of the Enemy," 89.

woman, a suburban housewife replete with a Vogue model's figure, a cliché of a station wagon, a mandatory child, a middle-class husband (obscurely at work in the city), and bags and bags of opulent groceries. It is this woman who sees the turn up ahead, *her* eyes which are "assaulted" by the swarming of hats and dresses. It is as if, by some miracle, a John Cheever character, absent-mindedly driving home from the supermarket, were to take a wrong turn and drive right into a documentary about the hungry hordes of migrant Mexicans—in authentic costumes, filmed on location. The number of patronizing assumptions embedded in the first paragraph is remarkable. But they are Annette's assumptions, and they affect her way of seeing, even as the action moves dramatically into gear.

A young Mexican boy jumps in front of her car, causing her to jam on the brakes; he fakes an accident by dropping below her line of vision—ah!—and scuttling to a ditch on the side. When the ruse is made clear, Annette and her son, both badly shaken, drive off amid the jeers of the Mexicans. Her food-laden station wagon (which they significantly miscall a Cadillac), her pristinely tailored self, her tidy child—all are a patent affront to these people. They answer it with mockery, with hate masquerading as fun. The whole scene, which takes up several pages, is densely packed with details of action, reaction—the perceived texture of heightened experience. There are many dashes—allowing the interpolation of added descriptive data—and a tendency to elide phrases, hurry syntax, crowd modifiers. Here is the description of the Mexican boy:

> The boy's thick black hair, curled with sweat, plastered onto his forehead, framed a delicate, cruelly tanned face, a face obviously dead white beneath its tan: great dark eyes, expanded out of proportion, neat little brows like angels' brows—that unbelievable and indecent beauty of children exploited for art—a pouting mouth, still purple at the corners from the raspberries picked and hidden for the long bus ride, these lips now turning as Annette stared into a hilarious grin and crying out at her and the stricken child who cringed beside her, legs already drawn up flatly at the knees. (p. 90)

One could not ask for a better example of high density and intensity.

But the reality warp of this story is fashioned from the peculiar kind of density and intensity typical of Oates's writing. The effect of her interpolations, her crammed modifiers, is to give an erratic speed to her syntax—to rush and then to retard our movement toward closure. The result is to create a prose that imitates the sensation of hypertensive consciousness. The same effect is created by the special kind of intensity she favors. The following list of phrases comes from the first three paragraphs of the story: "a dead dark blue," "yanked cruelly up," "station wagon moved in astonishment," "cruelly tanned face," "face . . . dead white," "indecent beauty," "in agony the brakes cried." Now, you may say this is just an overuse of the pathetic fallacy. It is, indeed. But in particular, she seems to be using the linguistic bonding of adjective-noun and verb-adverb to get away with impressionistic murder. Put more kindly, she is using it to join highly emotional and subjective qualities to the objects and events which make up her character's environment. In effect, she is bonding an overwrought consciousness with the here and now, this and that of circumstance. Are we to believe that we are seeing through the eyes of a mind that temperamentally and categorically distorts experience—or are we to believe that the author is simply heightening the crisis effect of the moment?

The grammar of expectation throws great emphasis on this question. We have to wonder who is seeing what we're being shown. The verb of our grammar is clear: it is simply "to attack," later qualified by "almost" and gradually softened to "threaten." But the dramatic impetus of the story comes from a further change in the verb and adverbs of the story sentence. We might record these changes as follows:

Annette (apparently) attacks (with the car) the Mexican boy.

Annette (symbolically) attacks (with her possessions) the Mexicans in the road, who stand for the workers in the field, the have-nots in the world.

Annette (actually) is attacked (with pebbles, a miniature stoning) by the Mexican boy.

Annette (in anticipation) is attacked (with intent to destroy) by the Mexicans near her home.

The shift from transitive to reflexive verb forms, from real to imagined conditions, defines the movement of the story from actual occurrence to paranoid response. What we need now is more knowledge of the subject. We need a who and a why clause.

Not until we have ridden home with her, not until we have seen how embarrassingly out of place that ranch-style home is, not until we have guessed how tenuous is the bond between mother and son, do we discover just who Annette is and why she is here. She is, we learn, a somewhat neurasthenic city woman who married out of insecurity, bore a child without wanting to, and is able to define herself only in terms of possessions. They tell us her position in life. Hers is a world of cultivated roses, sculptured drapes, and air conditioning—all at the control of a manicured finger.

After the incident on the way home, Annette is increasingly sure that the Mexicans are coming up the road to invade her property, to destroy her possessions. If we look for a pattern of linearity, we might find it in the series of entrenchments brought on by these "first views of the enemy." Thus, we would have a sequence something like this:

X_1: Retreating from the encounter in the road

X_2: Attempting to lock the gate (against the expected advance of the vengeful peasants)

X_3: Asserting command over her son Timmy (whose suspected identification with the Mexican boy is a threatening disaffection)

X_4: Drawing the drapes (thereby hiding from view the luxurious appointments of the house)

X_5: Closing windows

X_6: Clipping roses and stuffing them in vases (to "save" them from being ravaged and to fortify herself with "beauty")

X_7: Locking doors

X_8: Plying Timmy with strawberry tarts (to assert her possession of food and to win his allegiance away from the have-not Mexican child by gaining his complicity in the world of the haves)

The story does move along a path, along that road through (and symbolically over) the Mexicans, into the secure precincts of lawn and home, into the closed world of possessions, and finally into the furtive, febrile center of paranoia. "The enemy" are, of course, the creatures of her fear rather than the people she left in the road.

At the end of the story, we have these sentences:

> As if a secret ripened to bursting between them, swollen with passion, they smiled at each other. Timmy said, before biting into the tart, "*He* [the Mexican boy] can't hit the car again, it's all locked up." Annette said, gesturing at him with sticky fingers, "Here, darling. Eat this. Eat. *Eat*."
> (p. 102)

Almost repellently and perversely sensuous, that ending is itself over-ripe; it bursts under the repeated stabs of "Eat this. Eat. *Eat*." We're released from a pressure. In what way? Perhaps the typologies of closure can give us an insight here. For example, the physical sciences provide a paradigm for action equaled by reaction: a traumatic experience at the beginning of the story generates fear which takes the form of paranoid resistance. When the energy of that resistance equals the force of the initial experience, the story will end. Or take the behavioral sciences. We might say that Annette exhibits a form of obsessive-compulsive be-havior with a logic of its own. When she has carried out that logic to its natural conclusion, the story will end. The emotional period seems more important than any actual unit of time. Still, it is significant that the entire action takes place within the working-day period of the hus-band/father's absence. The story can last only so long as his return is postponed. But more pervasively, I think, we feel the closing in of neu-rosis, the final consequence of a tangled mess of guilt, confusion, fear— of social insularity, yes, but also of animal instinct (regarding territory, food, offspring) sheathed in a white linen dress.

When we apply the typology of genre, as Richter suggests, we can describe what is, to my mind, the central weakness of this undeniably powerful story. It is not a rhetorical fiction, because the symbolic refer-ents are not the point of the story; the sociological framework is pres-ent only to give grounds for and to enhance the psychological drama. But in fact Annette is a cut-out doll, to whom Oates has affixed just those qualities—in sketchiest detail—needed to give minimal credence to her protective massacre of roses, her desperate strawberry bribe. An-nette is patently a "type"—the overwrought wife and mother with all the middle-class accoutrements. She is, after all, not just a thin, but a "thin, fashionably thin young woman." The paranoia has substance only if we see Annette as an extreme case of the type. Yet the fiction expects us to take her to heart (mind? soul?) as a gaudily particular case of bad nerves.

When I think of this story poised between the extremes of incoherence, I do not see it securely integrated, somewhere in the middle (like "Order of Insects"), but rather as swinging rather dizzily between a fixated, compulsive repetitiveness (I must barricade, barricade, barricade) and the erratic flurry ("What should [I] do next?") of crazed sequentiality. Both the repetitions and the sequences emphasize that this is a homecoming story. Indeed, Annette is obsessively clinging to and retreating within her elaborate nest. But since the basis for at-homeness is her material possessions rather than any personal strength, her security is easily threatened, her balance upset. Clearly the rhythm here is an emotional one. It tempts us to look for primitive analogues. Perhaps, remembering Jarrell and the models of organic function, we might say the story resists and then yields closure much as the sphincter resists and then grants, at last, release. The story "contains" a spill of control.

"The Wheelbarrow," by V. S. Pritchett

Consider, for a moment, the difference between "Robert" and "Miss Freshwater's niece." Both are names, and both presumably "intend," or point to, specific individuals, one male and one female. Whoever the he and she are, one is being called informally by the first name (though not so casually as "Bob"), and the other is being referred to indirectly, as though her identity were to be routed through that of her aunt—and a freshwater "Miss," at that! Well, a social and sexual context—however minimal—is implied by those names. Should we now discover the "he" soliciting the "she," or the "she" commanding the "he," we'd know a great deal more. This is what we hear at the beginning of "The Wheelbarrow":

> "Robert," Miss Freshwater's niece called down from the window of the dismantled bedroom, "when you have finished that, would you mind coming upstairs a minute? I want you to move a trunk."[5]

5. Pritchett, "The Wheelbarrow," 22.

It is a very situational opening. Robert is outside, below; the niece is inside, above. He is someone she can give orders to, but in the form of a polite request—as if she isn't quite sure how far her authority extends. Furthermore, she can ask him to join her in a bedroom—but only to move a trunk; the intimacy is neutralized (we'll see it has not been eliminated) by the fact that the room is "dismantled," denatured, packed up.

This is the story of a middle-aged woman, who has had a restrictive, loveless childhood in the care of her aunt, and then an unwise marriage that ended in divorce. Yet this is also a woman who has never been locked into the proprieties by which her aunt lived, who has a certain free-and-easiness balanced by good common sense. She can be tough, a little prim, but basically, "lazy, smiling and drifting, she always [falls] on her feet." Learning that her aunt has died and willed her the family home, she returns to clean out the old house and get it ready for sale. In this task she has the unexpected but fortuitous help of a local taxi driver, who snares her at the station, grasps her situation quickly, sees (with charmingly disguised venality) "what's in it for him," and appoints himself to her service.

So this is a story about a woman's encounter with the detritus of the past, the relics which define her as "Miss Freshwater's niece." It is also about her encounter with an engaging Welshman, whose history of dissipation and habit of sermonizing (he is a converted sinner and a lay preacher of the most sanctimonious kind) yield an interesting mixture of brash opportunism, shrewd insight, friendly charm, sexual appeal, and amusing hypocrisy.

In the fine, rich tradition of English realism, Pritchett fills out the grammar of expectation in full detail. A woman (whom we know a great deal about) meets (in fully rendered circumstances) a man (whom we know enough about). Also, this same woman meets her past (which we learn quite a lot about). What will these two meetings, deftly intertwined, produce? Perhaps what is initially missing, or held in abeyance, is a refinement of the verb "to meet." Will she be abused or amused, cheated, enchanted, blessed or beguiled? Will she survive? And, if so, what are the terms of survival?

Pritchett uses description in a way that appears liberal, yet is in fact economical. Details of setting are imbued with suggestions of a way of living, habits of action, preferred values, quirks and customs. Dialogue is never stilled for long. The voices of these two people fill the story. The texture of the prose is only moderately dense; that is, it tends toward a simple syntax, with seldom more than one level of subordination. It is a fluid style that works with extreme efficiency without calling attention to itself. Here is a moment of relatively intense emotion:

> She did not hear him. Her face had drained of waking light. She had entered blindly into a dream in which she could hardly drag herself along. She was looking painfully through the album, rocking her head slowly from side to side, her mouth opening a little and closing on the point of speech, a shoulder rising as if she had been hurt, and her back moving and swaying as she felt the clasp of the past like hands on her. She was looking at ten forgotten years of her life, her own life, not her family's, and she did not laugh when she saw the skirts too long, the top-heavy hats hiding the eyes, her face too full and fat, her plainness so sullen, her prettiness too open-mouthed and loud, her look too grossly shy. (pp. 30–31)

Emotion is immediately embodied in concrete perceptions and actions that remain simple, empirical—even when evaluative, and even when figurative. "She felt the clasp of the past like hands on her." It is a clause that exploits neither the energies of language as such (except for the quiet chime of "clasp" and "past"), nor the range of originality in figures of speech; it neither sharpens nor exacerbates our sense of how memory acts on consciousness—much less on this particular mind. Yet placed back in its context, we can see this clause as one of twenty ordinary ropes all working together and inconspicuously to ply a sail to the wind. And the wind here is character. Not in the sense that Ahab is a character in *Moby-Dick*, but in the sense that my next-door neighbor is "quite a character." Miss Freshwater's niece is a woman who can repel a sexual invitation by "choosing a lugubrious tone." She is somebody who can be shaken by the memory of dead passions and then, seeing their emptiness, tear up their relics. She can be titillated by a charming rogue, do her share of the flirting—and then laugh when she sees that it was, after all, her wheelbarrow he wanted.

Linearity in this story is felt in the sequence of meetings with Robert. Each is a subtle play of shifting dominance—in the areas of social status, moral leverage, conversational wit, and sexual teasing. Later we'll see how chronology is altered, but here we will take these meetings in the order they are presented to the reader:

X_1: She calls Robert from the bedroom window and watches as he stops to admire the wheelbarrow he is using.

X_2: Robert "takes possession of her" at the station and appoints himself her handyman.

X_3: Robert begins his job by helping her dismantle the house, making wheelbarrow trips to the bonfire, and beginning the sexual byplay.

X_4: Robert joins her in the bedroom, where she reviews the aunt's clothes and discovers relics of her own past (which she "enters" as Robert watches and comments).

X_5: She joins Robert in the garden for tea, and learns of his past, withdraws from his advances, and gives him the wheelbarrow.

X_6: She overhears a portion of his sermon before leaving the village for good.

As we trace the course of these encounters, we see the potent anti-closure elements (we *can't* come to the end until we learn what the characters want, what each one will give, and what each one will get). But we also feel the impetus toward closure. We want the answers to those questions. And I think the movement is hastened by our feeling that the situation is familiar. A Welsh miner (turned cabby and preacher) is admitted to the garden, house, and family secrets of an unattached, school-teachery but rousable woman—well, you have almost a parody of the sort of story that brings a match to the wood. The outmoded rubbage, conveyed in the strident wheelbarrow, pushed by the virile Robert, does indeed end up on a literal pyre. But does our heroine burn in flames à la Lawrence?

From everything I have said so far, it should be evident that this is a very traditional story. It gives us fully rounded characters in settings described with mirror fidelity; it lets us see exactly what would happen if these characters acted "in character," in circumstances arranged exactly to test them. Yet as soon as that's said, I feel it isn't the point. Evans is a classic rogue—but his bold and devious love of the wheelbarrow is not part of the convention. His insinuating personalness is part of his charm, but not this spare, keen knowledge tailing off into the commonplace:

> "Old people are hungry. They are greedy. My grandmother nibbled like a little rat, all day. And in the night too. They wake up in the night and they are afraid. They eat for comfort. The mice did not get in, I hope," he said, going to look in the drawer. (p. 27)

Furthermore, we expect the sudden encounter with the past to produce a meditative, perhaps bitter, perhaps sentimental mood in the woman. We may even look for wry confessions to strangers. But do we expect the kindly taunting, the obscure happiness, the knowing humor that fills out our experience of this woman?

Thinking again about that conventional plot, we should realize the ways in which it does not move—or end—as expected. Two days are involved, but we do not follow their simple chronology. We begin at the open window, the call to Robert. She wants him to move a trunk. In other words, we begin at a moment of the second day, then go back to the arrival on the first day, then pick up at the open window again. From the bedroom scene (which in itself is a coy avoidance of other conventions, while yet calling them to mind), we move back into the past, then up through the garden scene. In standard terms, this is a seduction scene. He hints at his desire for her, touching her neck, waist, and knee. But suddenly the tables are turned and she is toying with his actual desire to get his hands on her wheelbarrow. Finally, with relenting kindness, she gives it to him.

Having gotten what he wants, he does not come back, and in short narrative order, we arrive at the end of her stay. Then the pace slows down for a final scene. Miss Freshwater's niece, sensible as she is, has been stirred by the adventure. After all, it has had its moments of camaraderie and excitement. She is about to leave for good, but she will go by way of the open-air church where Robert preaches every day. Her motives may be either intriguingly complex or embarrassingly simple. She wants, at any rate, to come within range again. Stop the story here and ask "how it ends," and any handful of students can give you the normative patterns. A man and a woman either match up or split up.

Yet, in fact, here is how the story ends: Robert's voice is coming over the loudspeaker. He cannot be seen, but he can be heard addressing the crowd on the theme of temptation. With beautiful and unscrupulous economy, he has turned the experience of the past two days into the text for his sermon. But he has made some changes. Instead of saying that he has been helping a woman burn old debris so as to get what he wanted for himself, he turns to parable:

> "Oh my friends, I was a slave of the strange woman the Bible tells about, the whore of Babylon, in her palace where moth and dust . . ."
>
> "And then by the great mercy of the Lord I heard a voice cry out, 'Robert Evans, what are you doing, boy? Come out of it' . . ."
>
> ". . . and burned the adulteress in the everlasting fire, my friends—and all her property."
>
> The hymn started up again.
>
> "Well not quite all, Robert," said Miss Freshwater's niece pleasantly aloud, and a child eating an ice-cream near her watched her walk across the grass to the bus stop.   (p. 40)

We have been reminded, finally, that the vision of this story is sanely, kindly, comic. This is a unit of discourse that coheres firmly despite the strong impetus of "now this and now that."

Story closure is signaled very obviously here by the word "stop." It is also achieved by the return to a depot, the closing of a visit "home." Yet because this visit has been effectively to destroy the claim of a repressive past, to get *away* from home, there is a feeling of an epoch ending. But what closes this story most definitely is a sufficiency of knowledge. Now we know all about Robert. The lengths he will go. His real—but still charming—hypocrisy. And now we know—and we'll probably nod rather than laugh or cry—that "Miss Freshwater's niece" has survived her name.

The Spectrum of Fiction

I began this chapter by assuming that all of my readers had found the way to the House of Usher, but that it was harder now to read the map of fiction. Perhaps we still read stories for the good old reason, to get to know people. We share the curiosity, though not the scruples, of Hawthorne's Peeping Tom—we want to visit in other peoples' lives without the bother of dressing up, being polite, or taking the consequences. In that case, we might ask what kind of people are "the wife of the house," "Miss Freshwater's niece," and the fearful Annette. Have we ever met anyone like them or do we believe that we might? Do we think of them as women we could call on the phone, if only we had the right phonebook?

These questions are certainly naïve, and yet I think each of the three stories I've examined does requite a love of gossip. Of course I've chosen stories that happen to do so. It was not my intention to illustrate a spectrum all the way from the very "nonrealistic" (avant garde, obscure) to the traditionally mimetic. Rather, I wished us to look at three different ways of creating a reality warp. If these stories create a spectrum, they do so by virtue of their different "intentions."[6] And if they tell us something about where modern short fiction is, they do so by changing our notions of what stories can do.

Gass's story "intends" the experience of an ontological awakening. But his story does not simply depict someone undergoing this enlightenment, nor does it produce an imitated event in the reader. The story creates a model of the experience, a model made out of words— words we might elsewhere encounter in our habits of speech, but find here reconditioned by the pressures of context.[7] Oh, the woman seems real enough, but that's not the point. She has only so much apparent verisimilitude (that is, she "intends" a woman we might call on the phone) only in those particulars and to that degree which completes the model—and lets us know that, in its creation, a human value is served. Our discussion of the "law" the story shows leads to an understanding of the story as a model, in fiction, of a principle of existence. The fiction is a metaphor for what we know to be true of the process of philosophical awareness. It is a "figure of life."

Does Oates's story work the same way? If I am right in thinking that Annette "intends" a class of human beings rendered excruciatingly particular in this instance—then it seems to me that the story is not offered as a "figure of life," but as a piece of it brought dripping to the page. But, no, not quite that either, for that would mean the story was merely an excision from life. As she has said, Oates is specifically interested in "the mystery of human emotions." No full explanation is possible; she is fascinated by that very fact. In "First Views of the Enemy," there

---

6. See Chapter Two.
7. See discussion of "constraints" in Chapter Two and elsewhere.

is a sequence of events that precipitates the fear of attack, but the response—at first an understandable reaction to the pebble-slinging—soon grows out of proportion to the stimulus. Such a statement, of course, assumes that readers have a sense of normative behavior; indeed, social cohesion, moral liability, and the definitions of insanity all require that such a sense prevail. But it seems to me that Oates wishes to short-circuit the question of sanity, to have us ask not what we think of this woman, but what we've shared with her during the story.

To say that Annette overreacts, to say that the language is overcharged with subjective conditioning, is to presume the existence of a normal reaction, a neutral language. However false, the presumption does exist as a working principle—just as we presume that subjects will usually precede verbs, that effects will come after causes, that defenses imply an attack. These presumptions are necessary to their effective violation, just as a normal breath rate is necessary to our knowledge of a sigh and a gasp. It seems to me that the language of this story is quite deliberately loaded, that it is meant to engage our attention with an immediacy and completeness that excludes all questions, all wandering thought, even—I would argue—all aesthetic appreciation of its own devices. It is meant to engross us in the act of postponing judgment. The story is not patently the model of a form of paranoia, nor is it an imitation, in words, of the distress it's about (though it may be both of these things to some extent). Like all stories, but with particular prominence here, it is an experience of intensified attention and reactivity, of dealing with multiplied and compressed acts of assimilation.

As I argued in an earlier chapter, we do not necessarily picture the referent of a closely packed bundle of concrete images; however, Oates stuffs in so many that they offer unusual resistance to closure. They also establish certain basic, orienting conceptions and emotional circuits—dust, vivid color, flesh, fear—as well as creating certain "spots of determinacy" (perhaps the angelic eyebrows of the Mexican boy) which reside in the mind, which are in effect mnemonic devices for the experience of the story. In short, neither character nor plot is so important as the argument of images, the logic of assault. The story induces, for the time of its duration, our acceptance of that logic—which we are actively accommodating ourselves to by the very act of grasping it. The story does what neither a psychiatric report nor a personal involvement could do—it normalizes the abnormal.

Now I am not suggesting that Oates wrote this story in order to trick us into tolerance, or even to prove that within the most normal mind (that of a middle-class housewife?), there is the potential for a mystery of emotion. I think she wants to give us a scare—to make us tremble at what we've accepted on the road through her story. I do think she wants us to feel our exposure the way a visionary feels his openness to God. We should know the story true the same way he knows his vision real— in other words, by an emotional acquiescence that is finally a mystery.

One would expect a more conservative aim in Pritchett. As I said in the discussion of his story, he is an old hand at the conventions of story. And truly, I think the point here *is* to get to know people—the way they sometimes foil expectation and yet always conform to it. The unobtrusive language, modestly at work, seems to behave very much as language should in the affairs of the world—to point our attention truly and precisely to something which would still exist if the pointer were dropped. And I do not for a moment underestimate the sensitivity to English syntax and diction, the infallible ear, and the love of words so evident here. It is easy to see the baroque opacity of language in Gass, harder to see—and to appreciate—its vital clarity in Pritchett.

I argued that "The Wheelbarrow" led us to a perception of the foibles and strengths of two highly individuated characters. We were certainly to keep in mind not only the norms of human nature (Robert has them firmly in mind), but also the conventions of fiction. And even more particularly, I should say, the convention of fiction as a filled-out version of drama on stage—a comedy of manners, to be yet more precise. In being even more exactly true to his or her own nature, each character comically anticipates, mistakes, and yet ironically triumphs over the nature of the other. What we experience is too empirical to "intend" an abstraction, a figure of life; it also encourages too much detachment to be an emotional bath. The critical faculties are joyously invoked, and while we are presented with two people who are amusingly distinct, if not quite eccentric, we feel the norms of a wise and worldly experience both illustrated and confirmed. The story gives us an opportunity to exercise a balance between sympathetic identification and critical distance, between emotional involvement and tough-minded insight. How often in our own lives do we experience such proportioned folly, such adequate sense? The story leaves us wearing an Olympian smile.

It is an easy step now to consider these stories as interruptions in our life. I'll ask you to recall the earlier discussions of the short story as a competitor with other rhythms of the day. I'll ask you, too, to think how great an advantage the story gains from the ruling power of the impetus to closure. For let me remind you of the nature of endings. First of all, there is physical closure, which comes when we've made our way, sentence by sentence, to the very last word. It is a kind of closure reached most comfortably with Pritchett, most taxingly with Gass. Immediate cognitive closure, the feeling that we know what we've read, may come most quickly with Oates. Yet even here, our fullest appreciation of meaning—deferred cognitive closure—won't come right away. With Pritchett, too, there may be a second's delay before we realize just how good-humored the heroine is. But it doesn't take us too long to see what she means when she says that not all of her property was burned in the flames. We know that Robert has no objections to at least one item of worldly goods—that wonderful wheelbarrow. Knowledge is what Gass's heroine gets, too—but an understanding so abstract and so circumscribed by the problems of using or maintaining it, that the ending is more of a stare than a wink.

In fact, I think it safe to say that deferred cognitive closure is most difficult in the Gass story because the philosophical issues it raises are more complex—and also, by the way, eternal. Perhaps we could substitute "psychological" for "philosophical" and say the same for the Oates story. Naturally, the resistance to deferred cognitive closure varies with the reader's experience and habits of thought. For me, the Gass story remains an object for evolving appreciation because of its intricate design and also because it hands over a theme that encourages thought. The Oates story leaves behind it, in my mind, some thought-provoking objections to its fictional practice and general presumptions. In contrast to both the Gass and Oates stories, the Pritchett story seems to offer little resistance to deferred cognitive closure. Of course it may prompt me to think further, but the thought is likely to be about realistic fiction, some people I know, or just human nature. I feel the urge to move from the story into life, or to retell the story as though I knew the principals, but I do not feel drawn back into the rhythm of the story itself.

Perhaps we have never finished with our discussion of a story until we can say where it leaves us, or, rather, to what it returns us as we reenter our lives. No doubt we all read stories sometimes, or always to some extent, to fill a gap or a lull in our lives. Perhaps we always expect to come away with our emotions stirred and our minds enlightened, to have, as we say, a vicarious experience. But when we say that, we are saying that the sun moves around the earth. We are being knowingly, conveniently, naïve. For the fact may be that contemporary short stories don't put us on the map—in the hills of the Hudson, the woods of New England, the houses of Usher—but instead put the world on a spin; a mystery of emotion, a comedy of desire, a calculus of being—these are just a few of the axes of fiction. They warp our reality, bend our minds to new truth.

Epilogue

• • •

If you have come with me this far, you will have been willing, perhaps, to share many assumptions that are rarely discussed in anthologies of short fiction. You will, perhaps, have agreed to consider my emphasis on the sentence unit and on the story unit or reality warp. Let me imagine that you have also shared with me a conviction that the elements and parts of short fiction are less important than its linearity and spatiality. Yet still it may be that much of what I have said seems true of fiction in general. Still you may wonder how much wiser we are as appreciators of short fiction. Has the nature of story slipped once more through our hands?

Yes—if we hoped for masking-tape labels. But perhaps not if we have been willing to make the most radical assumption of all. Short stories, unlike novels or poems, by their very nature, compete with the rhythms that keep us functioning as organisms. Stories complete themselves in our experience between other cycles of need—for food, sleep, and the releases of the body. Unlike longer fictions—even the most artful and word-conscious novels—short stories do not offer vicarious experience of a surrogate world. They haven't the time. Rather, as I have insisted all along, they put us *through* something—reality warp is the shorthand for it—that happens to us with as much authority as a delayed meal or an overdue nap. Our minds adjust to a frequency. Thus, we may be sluggish materialists, but while we read Gass we think philosophically. We may be skeptical rationalists, but while we read Oates, we reason in images, we think paranoically. And in reading Pritchett, we observe with amused acuity, we achieve a comic perspective. We can do any of these things for the space of a story.

So I've been suggesting that we ought no longer to ask first "What kind of story is this?" or "What are its elements?" or "How does it reflect the preoccupations of this author or this movement or this time?" These questions are important, of course, but my contention is that we already know how to ask them and how to make use of their answers. I'd also say that these questions can be asked of any fiction, long or short. If it is anything, this book is an argument for the primacy of a set of questions that apply uniquely to short stories: how do we get into, through, and out of a verbal experience that comes between meals? How is the reality warp created, and how does it make our minds behave while—and after—we're in it?

After all, I am simply arguing for a modernization of short story criticism, for taking into account the work of Formalists like Tzvetan Todorov and Victor Shklovsky, and of "reader-response" theorists like Wolfgang Iser and Stanley Fish. But most of all I am arguing for a new seriousness about short stories in the classroom as well as in the scholarly journals. In these times, when the mass media shape our imaginations in video segments, the nature and function of the art story is worth particular attention. We can hardly deny that narrative sequentiality is more potent in the TV script than in the liveliest story. Repeated images are surely more blatant in the recurring advertisement than in the most sensuous story. The recent televising of classic short fictions only makes more obvious the need for a reader-oriented criticism, if we are to determine, and preserve, what is unique about this form. Certainly contemporary writers of short fiction are well aware of the pressures they're under to give something different, something worthily taxing and genuinely memorable.

As readers, we should, I think, acknowledge the intensive demands that a good story makes. We should ask that the experience of the reality warp be worth the living time it displaces; as students we should task ourselves to describe linearities and densities and rhythms of closure. As critics, we may feel that such efforts are a labor of love. But we need a vocabulary for attentiveness. We have the responsibility for explaining why a given sequence of words takes us in and out of story.

Bibliography

• • •

Works of Fiction

Barth, John. "Lost in the Funhouse." In *Lost in the Funhouse*. Garden City, 1968.

Barthelme, Donald. "Sentence." In *City Life*. New York, 1970.

Bumpus, Jerry. "Our Golf Balls." In *Things in Place*. New York, 1975.

Carver, Raymond. "They're Not Your Husband." In *Will You Please Be Quiet, Please?* New York, 1976.

Chopin, Kate. "Athénaïse." In *The Complete Works of Kate Chopin*, edited by Per Seyersted. Vol. I of 2 vols. Baton Rouge, 1969.

Crane, Stephen. "The Open Boat." In *Tales of Adventure*. Charlottesville, 1969. Vol. V of *The University of Virginia Edition of the Works of Stephen Crane*, edited by Fredson Bowers. 10 vols.

Gass, William H. "Order of Insects." In *In the Heart of the Heart of the Country*. New York, 1968.

Gordimer, Nadine. "The Train from Rhodesia." In *Selected Stories*. New York, 1976.

Hawthorne, Nathaniel. "Roger Malvin's Burial." In *Mosses from an Old Manse*. Columbus, 1974. Vol. X of *The Centenary Edition of the Works of Nathaniel Hawthorne*. 14 vols.

Irving, Washington. "Rip Van Winkle." In *The Sketch Book of Geoffrey Crayon, Gent.* Boston, 1978.

Oates, Joyce Carol. "First Views of the Enemy." In *Upon the Sweeping Flood*. New York, 1966.

Poe, Edgar Allan. "The Murders in the Rue Morgue." In *Tales, Vol. III*.

1902; rpr. New York, 1965. Vol. IV of *The Complete Works of Edgar Allan Poe*, edited by James A. Harrison. 17 vols.

Porter, Katherine Anne. "Flowering Judas." In *The Collected Stories of Katherine Anne Porter*. New York, 1965.

Pritchett, V. S. "The Wheelbarrow." In *Selected Stories*. New York, 1978.

Works of Theory and Criticism

Adams, Robert M. "Romantic Openness and the Unconscious." In *Strains of Discord: Studies in Literary Openness*. Ithaca, 1958.

Allen, Walter. *The Short Story in English*. New York, 1981.

Arms, George. "Kate Chopin's *The Awakening* in the Perspective of Her Literary Career." In *Essays on American Literature in Honor of Jay B. Hubbell*, edited by Clarence Gohdes. Durham, 1967.

Backus, Joseph M. "'He Came Into Her Line of Vision Walking Backward': Non-sequential Sequence-Signals in Short Story Openings." *Language Learning*, XV, nos. 1 and 2 (1965), pp. 67–83.

Bader, A. L. "The Structure of the Modern Short Story." 1945; rpr. in *Short Story Theories*, edited by Charles E. May. Athens, Oh., 1976.

Baker, Carlos. "Delineation of Life and Character [in the Works of Kate Chopin]." In *Literary History of the United States*, edited by Robert E. Spiller. Vol. I of 3 vols. New York, 1948.

Balakian, Nona, and Charles Simmons, eds. *The Creative Present: Notes on Contemporary Fiction*. Garden City, 1963.

Baldeshwiler, Eileen. "'The Grave' as Lyrical Short Story." *Studies in Short Fiction*, I, 216–21.

———. "Katherine Mansfield's Theory of Fiction." *Studies in Short Fiction*, VII, 421–32.

———. "The Lyric Short Story: The Sketch of a History." 1969; rpr. in *Short Story Theories*, edited by Charles E. May. Athens, Oh., 1976.

——— [Sister M. Jocelyn, O.S.B.]. "Sherwood Anderson and the Lyric Story." In *The Twenties: Poetry and Prose*, edited by Richard E. Langford and William E. Taylor. Deland, Fla., 1966.

Bates, H. E. *The Modern Short Story: A Critical Survey*. Boston, 1941.

———. "The Modern Short Story: Retrospect." 1941; rpr. in *Short Story Theories*, edited by Charles E. May. Athens, Oh., 1976.

Beck, Warren. "Art and Formula in the Short Story." *College English*, V, 55–62.

Bender, Bert. "Kate Chopin's Lyrical Short Stories." *Studies in Short Fiction*, XI, 257–66.

Bender, Hans. "International Symposium on the Short Story, Part Two [West Germany]." *Kenyon Review*, 1st Ser., XXXI, 85–92.

Bennet, James R. "The Beginning and Ending: A Bibliography." *Style*, X, 184–88.

Bowen, Elizabeth. *After-Thought: Pieces About Writing*. London, 1962.
———. "The Faber Book of Modern Short Stories." 1936, 1950; rpr. in *Short Story Theories*, edited by Charles E. May. Athens, Oh., 1976.

Brown, E. K. *Rhythm in the Novel*. Montreal, 1950.

Canby, Henry Seidel, and Alfred Dashiell. *A Study of the Short Story*. Rev. ed. New York, 1935.

Cassola, Carlo. "International Symposium on the Short Story, Part One [Italy]." *Kenyon Review*, 1st Ser., XXX, 486–90.

Christensen, Francis. *Notes Toward a New Rhetoric*. New York, 1967.

Cowley, Malcolm. "Storytelling's Tarnished Image." *Saturday Review*, September 25, 1971, pp. 25–27, 54.

Crews, Frederick C. "The Logic of Compulsion in 'Roger Malvin's Burial.'" *PMLA*, LXXIX, 19–36.

DeLaura, David J. "Some Victorian Experiments in Closure." *Studies in the Literary Imagination*, VIII, 19–36.

Dollerup, Cay. "Concepts of 'Tension,' 'Intensity,' and 'Suspense' in Short-Story Theory." *Orbis Litterarum: International Review of Literary Studies* (Copenhagen), XXV, 314–37.

Dondore, Dorothy A. "Kate O'Flaherty Chopin." In *Dictionary of American Biography*. Vol. IV of 10 vols. 1929–30; rpr. New York, 1957–58.

Donohue, A. M. "'From Whose Bourne No Traveller Returns': A Reading of 'Roger Malvin's Burial.'" *Nineteenth-Century Fiction*, XVIII, 1–19.

Eble, Kenneth. "A Forgotten Novel: Kate Chopin's *The Awakening*." *Western Humanities Review*, X, 261–69.

Elkin, Stanley. "The Art of Fiction." *Paris Review*, LXVI, 55–86.

Erlich, Gloria C. "Guilt and Expiation in 'Roger Malvin's Burial.'" *Nineteenth-Century Fiction*, XXVI, 377–89.

Fletcher, Marie. "The Southern Woman in the Fiction of Kate Chopin." *Louisiana History*, VII, 117–32.

Frank, Joseph. "Spatial Form in Modern Literature." *Sewanee Review*, LIII, 221–40, 433–56, 643–53.

Freedman, Ralph. *The Lyric Novel*. Princeton, 1963.

Friedman, Alan. *The Turn of the Novel*. New York, 1966.

Friedman, Norman. *Form and Meaning in Fiction*. Athens, Ga., 1975.

Gass, William H. *Fiction and the Figures of Life*. New York, 1971.

———. Preface to paperback edition of *In the Heart of the Heart of the Country*. New York, 1976.

———. "A Symposium on Fiction [interview]." *Shenandoah*, XXVII, 3–31.

———. *The World Within the Word*. New York, 1978.

[Gibson, William M.]. "Love in Louisiana: Kate Chopin, a Forgotten Southern Novelist." Review of *Kate Chopin: A Critical Biography*, by Per Seyersted, and *The Complete Works of Kate Chopin*, edited by Per Seyersted. London *Times Literary Supplement*, October 9, 1970, p. 1163.

Gohdes, Clarence. "Exploitation of the Provinces." In *Literature of the American People*, edited by Arthur Hobson Quinn. New York, 1951.

Gordimer, Nadine. "The Flash of Fireflies." 1968; rpr. in *Short Story Theories*, edited by Charles E. May. Athens, Oh., 1976.

Gross, Beverly. "The Poetic Narrative: A Reading of 'Flowering Judas.'" *Style*, II, 129–39.

Gullason, Thomas A. "The Short Story: An Underrated Art." 1964; rpr. in *Short Story Theories*, edited by Charles E. May. Athens, Oh., 1976.

Harte, Bret. "The Rise of the Short Story." *Cornhill Magazine*. 3rd Ser., VII (July, 1899), pp. 1–8.

Hutchens, Eleanor N. "An Approach Through Time." In *Towards a Poetics of Fiction*, edited by Mark Spilka. Bloomington, 1977.

Ingarden, Roman. *The Literary Work of Art: An Investigation on the Borderlines of Ontology, Logic, and Theory of Literature*. Translated by George G. Grabowicz. Evanston, 1973.

Janeway, Elizabeth, ed. "Is the Short Story Necessary?" In *The Writer's World*. New York, 1969.

Jarrell, Randall. "Stories." From *The Anchor Book of Stories*. 1958; rpr. in *Short Story Theories*, edited by Charles E. May. Athens, Oh., 1976.

Kempton, Kenneth Payson. *The Short Story*. Cambridge, Mass., 1954.

Kenner, Hugh. *Studies in Change: A Book of the Short Story*. Englewood Cliffs, 1965.

Kermode, Frank. "An Approach Through History." In *Towards a Poetics of Fiction*, edited by Mark Spilka. Bloomington, 1977.

———. *The Sense of an Ending: Studies in the Theory of Fiction*. New York, 1967.

Kligerman, Jack. "A Stylistic Approach to Hawthorne's 'Roger Malvin's Burial.'" *Language and Style*, IV, 188–94.

Lawrence, James Cooper. "A Theory of the Short Story." 1917; rpr. in *Short Story Theories*, edited by Charles E. May. Athens, Oh., 1976.

Leary, Lewis. "Kate Chopin's Other Novel." *Southern Literary Journal*, I, 60–74.

Liebman, Sheldon, W. "'Roger Malvin's Burial': Hawthorne's Allegory of the Heart." *Studies in Short Fiction*, XII, 253–60.

Lovejoy, D. S. "Lovewell's Fight and Hawthorne's 'Roger Malvin's Burial.'" *New England Quarterly*, XXVII, 527–31.

Magliola, Robert R. *Phenomenology and Literature: An Introduction*. West Lafayette, Ind., 1977.

Matthews, Brander. *The Philosophy of the Short-Story*. New York, 1901.

May, Charles E., ed. *Short Story Theories*. Athens, Oh., 1976.

McCullen, J. T. "Ancient Rites for the Dead and Hawthorne's 'Roger Malvin's Burial.'" *Southern Folklore Quarterly*, XXX, 313–22.

Moravia, Alberto. "The Short Story and the Novel." 1969; rpr. in *Short Story Theories*, edited by Charles E. May. Athens, Oh., 1976.

Moss, Howard, ed. *The Poet's Story*. New York, 1973.

Oates, Joyce Carol. "The Short Story." *Southern Humanities Review*, V, 213–14.

O'Brien, Edward J. *The Advance of the American Short Story*. Rev. ed. New York, 1931.

O'Donovan, Michael [Frank O'Connor]. *The Lonely Voice: A Study of the Short Story*. Cleveland, 1963.

———. "The Lonely Voice." 1963; rpr. in *Short Story Theories*, edited by Charles E. May. Athens, Oh., 1976.

Orians, G. H. "The Source of 'Roger Malvin's Burial.'" *American Literature*, X, 313–18.

Patrick, Max, ed. *Style, Rhetoric, and Rhythm: Essays by Morris W. Croll*. Princeton, 1966.

Pattee, Fred Lewis. *The Development of the American Short Story*. New York, 1923.

———. *A History of American Literature Since 1870*. New York, 1915.

Peden, William. *The American Short Story: Continuity and Change, 1940–1975*. 2nd ed. Boston, 1975.

———. "The American Short Story in the Twenties." *Studies in Short Fiction*, X, 367–71.

Rankin, Daniel S. *Kate Chopin and Her Creole Stories*. Philadelphia, 1932.

Reid, Ian. *The Short Story*. New York, 1977.

Richter, David H. *Fable's End: Completeness and Closure in Rhetorical Fiction*. Chicago, 1974.

Robillard, Douglas. "Hawthorne's 'Roger Malvin's Burial.'" *Explicator*, XXVI, Item #56.

Rohrberger, Mary. "The Short Story: A Proposed Definition." 1966; rpr. in *Short Story Theories*, edited by Charles E. May. Athens, Oh., 1976.

Ross, Danforth. *The American Short Story*. Minneapolis, 1961.

Russell, John. "James Joyce's Sentences [in *Dubliners*]." *Style*, VI, 260–93.

Said, Edward W. *Beginnings: Intention and Method*. New York, 1975.

Saroyan, William. "International Symposium on the Short Story, Part Two [United States]." *Kenyon Review*, 1st Ser., XXXI, 58–62.

Schulz, Dieter. "Imagination and Self-Imprisonment: The Ending of 'Roger Malvin's Burial.'" *Studies in Short Fiction*, X, 183–86.

Seyersted, Per. *Kate Chopin: A Critical Biography*. Baton Rouge, 1969.

Slate, J. E. "William Carlos Williams and the Modern Short Story." *Southern Review*, New Ser., IV, 647–64.

Smith, Barbara H. *Poetic Closure: A Study of How Poems End*. Chicago, 1968.

Spilka, Mark, ed. *Towards a Poetics of Fiction*. Bloomington, 1977.

Stead, Christina. "International Symposium on the Short Story, Part One [England]." *Kenyon Review*, 1st Ser., XXX, 443–50.

Stroud, Theodore A. "A Critical Approach to the Short Story." 1956; rpr. in *Short Story Theories*, edited by Charles E. May. Athens, Oh., 1976.

Summers, Hollis. *Discussions of the Short Story*. Boston, 1963.

Thompson, W. R. "The Biblical Sources of Hawthorne's 'Roger Malvin's Burial.'" *PMLA*, LXXVII, 92–96.

Todorov, Tzvetan. *The Poetics of Prose*. Translated by Richard Howard. Ithaca, 1977.

Tompkins, Jane P., ed. *Reader-Response Criticism: From Formalism to Post-Structuralism*. Baltimore, 1980.

Welty, Eudora. *The Eye of the Story: Selected Essays and Reviews*. New York, 1978.

———. "The Reading and Writing of Short Stories." 1949; rpr. in *Short Story Theories*, edited by Charles E. May. Athens, Oh., 1976.

West, Ray B., Jr. *The Short Story in America, 1900–1950*. Chicago, 1952.

Whipple, Leonidas Rutledge. ["Kate Chopin"]. In *Library of Southern Literature*, edited by Edwin A. Alderman and Joel Chandler Harris. Vol. II of 16 vols. New Orleans, 1908–1913.

White, William M. "Hawthorne's Eighteen-Year Cycle: Ethan Brand and Reuben Bourne." *Studies in Short Fiction*, VI, 215–18.

Ziff, Larzar. *The American 1890's: Life and Times of a Lost Generation*. New York, 1966.

Index

• • •